You've Got This!

KEYS TO EFFECTIVE PARENTING
FOR THE EARLY YEARS

Simple Tools to Help Parents and Children
Feel Calm, Secure, and Confident

CHRISTINE KYRIAKAKOS MARTIN

outskirts
press

CONTENTS

DEDICATION

This book is dedicated to all early childhood professionals and teachers who have devoted their careers to facilitating children in healthy growth and development. It is also for all parents who spend a lifetime loving and nurturing their children to be caring and responsible individuals with integrity and good character.

On a personal note, this book is dedicated to many family members, students, parents, and colleagues that have taught me so much about the importance of investing in the lives of young children.

To my father, James Kaltsas, who taught me about family, love, and kindness. He believed in me and gave me the opportunity to open Sunshine Preschool when I was 24 years old. And to my mother, Sophie, who was the model of a strong woman. She taught me values to live by and that education was the most powerful tool.

To the amazing and nurturing staff, past and present, at Sunshine Preschool in Hopkinton, MA. They continue to be the best facilitators of a young child's total growth and development and have opened up worlds of learning and discovery for so many children over the years.

To my husband, Jim, who has always supported my dreams and life adventures with unconditional love and support, not just for me, but also for our entire family.

To my children, Nick, Jamie, and Ashley...you have rocked my world! Every day with you is a gift as I've watched you grow from children into the amazing individuals you are today. Nick: You have always showed your strength and persistence to accept challenges. Your smile radiates your inner self and your sensitive nature. You never cease to amaze me with all that you have done in your personal and professional career. Jamie: You are a loyal son, brother, and friend to all. Your warm personality resonates with everyone around you. You are creative, driven, and successful in meeting all the goals you set for yourself. Ashley: Your kind and peaceful nature brings calm to everyone around you. You have always let your heart guide you to wonderful things with your family and friends.

To my grandson, Austin: You melt my heart with your warmth and kind spirit. And to my future grandchildren: Yiayiá is waiting to share the love. My wish is that you all explore the world around you and see that there is so much to learn. Give, love, and live!

This book is also dedicated to the memory of one of my dearest friends, Diane Tsoules Fitzpatrick. Diane was a former special needs teacher who instilled the values of kindness, empathy, and love to all her family and students. Her children - Athena, Matthew, and Nicole - continue to be a big part of my life and they exhibit their mother's most beautiful qualities in their everyday lives.

To my siblings, family, and dear friends: Thank you all for standing with me and giving me so much encouragement through the years. To all the children of my friends and my children's friends who have been a part of my family, thank you, especially for the smiles and laughter I experienced being around you through your childhoods and into today!

And, of course, I can't forget to thank the thousands of children who started their first schooling experiences at Sunshine Preschool. I'd also like to thank their parents for valuing quality care and a sound early education philosophy. I am honored that you entrusted Sunshine Preschool with the care of your children. It has been a joy and pleasure to help these children and families enjoy and embrace the early childhood years.

This is for all of you.

C.K.M., 2018

INTRODUCTION

Parents, have you ever just had the worst day ever? Work was demanding, but when you go to pick up your child from preschool, you realize your bad day is far from over. You now have a new set of demands placed upon you from your child and you're beginning to feel like an "emotional hostage" within your own family. You know you don't spend enough time playing with your little one because of your work schedule and responsibilities around the home. You feel guilty because of stress, financial issues, a divorce…or just because you were running late and screamed at your preschooler for spilling milk as you were trying to run out the door this morning!

These stressors make you want to hit the drive-through for dinner, buy that toy your child has been whining about for weeks, or agree to a much-too-late bedtime. You find yourself agreeing to requests that are not normally on your radar. And why? Just for a moment of peace to make your bad day feel a bit better…for yourself and your child. You don't want a power-struggle, whining, or back talk. But you also don't feel like you have the time for a normal, pleasant conversation. You're in no state to be an encourager, a listener, a nurturer, a nurse...or even a great parent right now! You are exhausted, frustrated, overwhelmed, and stressed out...and it's YOU who wants a hug and to be cuddled just for a few moments. You need to get your energy back, your self-esteem boosted, and reclaim the joy you felt when you first held your child in your arms.

For over 40 years, I have listened to parents share a range of emotions just like these as they've raised their young children. I have experienced these moments myself. Parenting is the best and most rewarding experience of one's life...but it can also be the hardest and most confusing. It is not an easy job, it gets exhausting, and it's hard to be consistent, let alone calm. Life just gets in the way. But I'm here to tell you it's ok.

This book was written for you...the parent of a young child that needs a little help or just some practical encouragement. I want you to know, in the midst of your hardest days, there are ways to make things better! Sometimes these things are incredibly simple, but can make a world of difference for your family. I also want to remind you that YOU are the source of firsts for your young child: a teacher, cheerleader, coach, and shoulder to cry on. And your young child needs you in these critical first years of life. Ninety percent of the brain develops by age 5, and during these years, the brain is the most flexible and adaptable in making a strong impact on social, emotional, and cognitive learning abilities. I believe with the power of education and support, you can go from being the overwhelmed parent that wants to hide under the covers to the effective parent that can empower their children to be the best they can be.

This book is structured topically, covering some of the most pressing issues and questions brought up by parents in the 40+ years I've worked in the field of early childhood education. Each topic is then followed by practical tips, ways to apply the information within your own home, and quotes from individuals from a multitude of backgrounds (teachers, education specialists, parents, grandparents, and successful professionals) to provide you with encouragement and inspiration. Don't worry…you've got this!

Although I've learned a lot, seen a lot, and conducted extensive research in the field, I've found that it's also essential for parents to trust their gut and do what feels right for their individual children. A sense of humor doesn't hurt either; sometimes, for both parents and children, laughter is the best relief! I've tried to incorporate a lot of humor in these pages to remind you to take time to relax and laugh each day.

I know you can do this! Use the tools in this book to take a ride through the beautiful journey parenting can be. It's a ride that you take with the best possible passengers…your children.

"We as parents know how important early education is and the incredible impact it has on our children and their future success in schools. Hopkinton Public Schools have been highly rated in Massachusetts and nationally because so many residents believe in the value of education starting with a quality preschool. Our thanks to Sunshine Preschool and Mrs. Martin for her expertise, philosophy, and core values of early education."

- Kevin and Gabriela Dunn, Parents of Two Sons

ATTACHMENT AND BONDING

How strong connections can lead your child to social, emotional, and scholastic success

Have You Been There? It's hard to keep it together. The stress you feel at work and at home is making you crazy. You're anxious, overwhelmed, and on edge, even taking this out on your kids at times. You find that you don't have time to play with them much anymore because there's so much else needs to get done.

In their book, <u>Social & Emotional Development</u>, Dave Riley, Robert San Juan, and Ann Ramminger state that young children greatly benefit from secure attachments with adults and can suffer when these attachments become strained.[i] Secure attachments are created when an adult routinely meets the needs of a child in order to relieve that child's anxiety or fears. Children need to be able to engage in emotional and meaningful exchanges with their parents in a way that allows them to feel safe, heard, and emotionally connected. When children don't get these interactions with their parents (due to changes within the household, everyday stress, or some other shift in the family dynamic), they are more likely to feel disconnected, confused, anxious, and insecure.

The authors state, "Researchers have followed children from infancy to adulthood and find that having a secure attachment to at least one adult in the earliest years predicts better social relationships and better intellectual development in the years ahead."[ii] They point out that secure at-home relationships are essential, but so are secure attachments between young children and caregivers in early education settings: "...four year olds who were securely attached to their current teacher engaged in more complex play, were friendlier, and were less aggressive with peers..." and "...secure attachment with their very first early childhood teachers was a strong predictor of positive relationships with their elementary school teachers and peers."[iii]

A child's strong attachment to parents, grandparents, or first caregivers can make a powerful impact on that child's social-emotional skills and overall academic abilities. A secure attachment or bond allows the child to feel safe, protected, and confident to explore their world and learn new things. And, as mentioned above, it's also essential that children in early education programs feel a secure attachment to their teachers.

As a parent, grandparent, and preschool director I have seen that more time spent with the same caregiver actually enhances a child's secure attachments, especially if the child isn't experiencing strong bonds within the home. Overall, strong bonds between children and adult caregivers provide the safety and confidence needed for healthy development and overall academic success.

***

YOU'VE GOT THIS!

Have Daily Uninterrupted Interaction - Designate time (15 minutes or longer) for your eyes and ears to be completely focused on your child each day. Don't use technology, videos, or cell phones to occupy the time. See and hear your child's need for a hug, story, song, or just simple playtime for the two of you. Even if things get busy, just focus on spending at least 15 minutes together…preferably more!

Ask Your Child More Questions - Open the lines of communication by asking questions that might spark your child's interest. Try "What's your favorite toy right now?" or "Is there something new you would like to learn or try?" You might be surprised at your child's answers!

Be Present and Calm - A peaceful demeanor will not only help you listen more to your child's needs, but will help your child feel more secure and connected while in your presence. Take a deep breath, smile, and show your child that no matter what is happening in your life, you'll always be there for him or her.

***

"In my life, loved ones, friends, and significant others have come and gone. It has always left me feeling a bit insecure about the next relationship...but the parental style of my mother left me with one certainty in life: She will always be there for me, no matter what the circumstances. In such an insecure and unsure world, the unconditional love given to me by my mother became a constant in my heart. It allowed me a confidence to face fears and obstacles knowing that no matter what happens, she will be there for me."
- Nick, Telecom Director

"Losing my mom when she was 52 sent me in a spiral early on, but she had always prepared me for life without her. Not that it would be easy, but that there would always be love all around me. Between my blood relatives, her closest friends, the mothers of my best friends, and my sisters, I had countless strong and caring women to look up to. Not a day goes by that I don't think about my mom and the lessons she tried to impart: work hard, be kind, love your family, and the rest will work itself out."
- Matthew, Director of Ticket Services & Technology

4

BEDTIME

Why creating a proper environment for sleep
can help children (and adults) get better rest

> *"Without enough sleep, we all become tall two
> year olds."* - JoJo Jensen

Sleep is vital for young children...and their parents as
well. Any mom or dad of a young child knows that, without
enough sleep, days can feel particularly long and taxing.
That's why a solid bedtime routine is of paramount
importance. In fact, a lack of sleep can adversely impact
proper development and cause issues like more frequent
illness, a decrease in academic achievement, an inability
to focus, slower reaction times, and a regression in
coordination.[iv]

In order to avoid the negative effects that a lack of
sleep can induce, think about some of the reasons
children often have a hard time going to bed in the first
place: parents may not understand the sleep needs of
their child, they may not have established a set routine
with predictable tasks and a solid bedtime, the child may
get over-stimulated before trying to fall asleep, or changes

within the home or the child's life may be contributing to a disruption in normal sleep patterns. If you can identify the source of the child's poor sleep, it's much easier to craft a solution (such as introducing a new bedtime routine, eliminating television or technology in the evenings, or giving the child more quality time to discuss life changes).

There are plenty of ways to create an environment that promotes restful sleep within your home. These actually start, not when your child crawls into bed at night, but rather when he or she wakes. Try to get your child up at the same time each day. Then, throughout the day, make sure that outside influences aren't responsible for poor sleep. Such influences could include caffeine (which lurks in soda, chocolate, and even some medicines), an over-scheduled day, or too much time in front of a TV or screens. Then, in the evening, create consistent and predictable tasks to prepare your child for rest like teeth brushing, a goodnight book, and lights out at the same time each night. With consistency, bedtime will become a much calmer experience when the home environment adapts to helping them sleep better.

If bedtimes are particularly troubling for you and your child, read on for specific strategies to help with particular bedtime-related issues:

***

YOU'VE GOT THIS!

Understand Your Child's Particular Sleep Needs - Many child development professionals believe that infants should get up to 17 hours of sleep per day, with toddlers and preschoolers needing 11 to 12 hours per day.[v] Is your child sleeping long enough to meet these needs? If not, start the bedtime routine 15 minutes earlier for a few days, then 30 minutes, then an hour (if necessary) until your child is getting adequate sleep throughout the night.

Your Child May Need More Time With You - Sometimes at the end of the day, parents can be so tired and ready for some "alone time" that they rush to get their child tucked in. But often, this rush can make children feel pushed to the side. This may create situations where children can't calm down or continue to get out of bed frequently. Instead of rushing, start the bedtime routine earlier (allowing for ample quality time with the child before the lights go out), create meaningful rituals together (with songs, hugs, kisses, prayers, or just a short time to talk about the day), and lay out clear expectations for the child (like, "You may not come out of your bedroom unless there is an emergency, and if you do, I will take you back to bed").

Offer Choices To Give Children Control - Sometimes bedtime problems are simply power struggles between children and their parents. Children may just want to challenge what is happening. And, since emotions can often be heightened at bedtime, this can lead to significant and lengthy clashes. If your child desires more control over this time of the day, offer him or her choices to become more involved in the bedtime routine. For example, allow your child to choose his or her pajamas, books, special blankets, pillows, or a stuffed animal. By allowing your child to make decisions within the routine, you are helping him or her feel valued and a part of the process. This not only helps the child feel more responsible, but ultimately more self-assured and confident.

When Nothing Else Works… - If no solutions seem to be working and your child won't stay in bed, get a folding chair and try this: If your child gets out of bed after the nightly routine is complete, bring the child back to his or her bed. Do not lie down with your child, but just sit next to him or her in the chair. Move the chair further away from the bed each time, eventually by the door, then in the hall. It may seem like a long process until the child transitions and trusts that he or she is safe, but consistency and follow through will likely work...and you'll both be sleeping better!

CHALLENGING
BEHAVIORS

How parents can teach children
positive social interactions to overcome
disruptive or aggressive behaviors

> *"Challenging behavior is just a signal, the fever, the means by which the kid is communicating that he or she is having difficulty meeting an expectation."*
> - Ross W. Greene

The National Institute for Early Education Research (NIEER) defines a challenging behavior as, "...any repeated pattern of behavior that interferes with learning or engagement in social interactions."[vi] These behaviors can include tantrums, verbal aggression, disruptive behavior, noncompliance, or withdrawal. Behaviors like these can interfere with the child's development, bring harm to other children or adults, and put the child at high risk for future social and academic problems. But it is possible to help children with challenging behaviors grow into well-adjusted, self-assured individuals. It just takes some extra time, patience, and guidance.

First, parents must remember to be more reflective than reactive when it comes to seeing progress with challenging behaviors. This starts with considering the factors that may be contributing to these behaviors in the first place. Are there biological factors at play (like a difficult temperament, neurological issues, developmental or language delays, or mental illness)? Is the child's environment a contributor; has he or she been exposed to violence, absorbed too much media, or experienced a change within the home structure? Or is the child getting something out of this behavior, like attention, access to something, or getting out of something he or she doesn't want to do? Before you can figure out how to alter challenging behaviors, you must first do the reflective work to recognize their source. In doing this work, don't place blame on the source, but use this process to gather more information about your child's individual needs.

Next, it's important to focus on the elements within the child's environment that you can influence. Are there any triggers that you can immediately eliminate within the environment? Does your child need to be reminded to use more pro-social actions before entering into a social situation? Do you need to help him or her become more confident and self-assured? Your goal should be to try to boost your child's resilience to overcome challenging behaviors before they become a negative pattern that's harder to correct.

Remember, it can take a while for a child to change behavior patterns, and this becomes almost impossible without assistance from a caring adult. But, with consistency and patience, it is possible for negative and challenging behaviors to decrease.

***

YOU'VE GOT THIS!

Intervene Early - Parents need to use preventative methods early, before a challenging behavior occurs. Don't wait for your child to make a mistake. Remind him or her of ways to handle problems before these behaviors even take place. Children need these reminders in order for positive social patterns to be embedded in their brains and eventually become their "go-to" for handling conflict and upset.

Be Consistent - Because challenging behaviors can be so persistent, consistency in supporting a child's improvement is important. Even though you may feel like little change is happening as you attempt to lead your child towards more pro-social behaviors, remember that change takes a lot of time and effort. But as you maintain consistency, you are actually helping to effectively create new brain networks for your child's future years.

Don't Avoid Social Interactions - Parents with children exhibiting challenging behaviors might want to avoid putting them in social situations to eliminate conflict, but this may do more harm than good. In order to learn pro-social skills, children need to be in environments where they can practice navigating social interactions and improve their responses with the help of caring adults. When parents can support and nurture these interactions, they help children see more productive ways to handle their difficult feelings.

If Needed, Ask for Help - In particularly challenging situations, when a child may do harm to him or herself or others, parents may need support from medical professionals, therapists, or counselors. NIEER states that these professionals can work with parents to distinguish a child's comprehensive needs in order to prepare them to succeed in school and in life.[vii]

***

"Consistency at school and at home, when a challenging behavior comes up, is very important. Setting up a routine, scheduling work and play, and then making a chart together with your child allows him or her to have input. At first it will take many reminders and at the onset there will be setbacks, but if you stick with it and have positive reinforcements consistently, things should improve."
– Robin, Special Needs Chairperson

CONSEQUENCES

How effective consequences can teach your child important lessons about responsibility and accountability

Have You Been There? The movie is starting in 30 minutes but your daughter refuses, after repeated requests from you, to put on her shoes. This leads you to say, "If you don't put your shoes on right now, we aren't going to the movie." This is a total bluff since you've already made plans to meet some friends at the theater, but you can't think of anything else to say to get her moving. When she continues to sit in defiance, you just put her shoes on her feet and carry her to the car. You're frustrated, but you don't want to cancel your plans for the afternoon.

Parents can often threaten consequences that they don't necessarily mean because they're stressed out or frustrated. I've heard parents threaten, "I'm throwing all of your toys away when we get home," when a young child cries over not being able to get a new action figure at the store. But I highly doubt this threat is ever carried out when the family gets home. And I've never seen a child calm down or change his or her behavior when parents say they're going to hand out an over-the-top consequence. In fact, it can make the behavior even worse!

When parents threaten consequences, then don't follow through on them, it sends children the message that it doesn't really matter if they listen, cooperate, or comply because their mom and dad aren't actually going to follow through with any discipline. And when this happens, children don't learn the lessons that consequences can teach about making better choices and being responsible for their actions. So how can parents use consequences they can stick with?

First, it's important to think about the types of consequences that will make the most sense for the situation. Many times, a child will experience a consequence of his or her own behavior without you having to do anything at all. This is called a natural consequence and happens, for example, when a child won't put on rain boots and then gets cold and wet feet. Natural consequences, because they happen through direct experience, can sometimes teach children quicker than other consequences that parents hand out. But if you need to impose a consequence to discourage undesirable behavior, try to make it a logical consequence that fits the circumstance. The Raising Children Network provides these examples: 'If a child is being silly and spills her drink, she must wipe it up,' and 'If a bike is left in the driveway, it gets put away for the rest of the afternoon.'[viii] In these examples, the consequence fits the situation and provides the child with the opportunity to consider the issue and think about how to change his or her behavior the next time.

Consistency is also a key component to effective consequences. When parents and children map out clear expectations and talk about consequences before they have to be handed out, things generally run much more smoothly. The Raising Children Network states, "If children clearly understand what you expect them to do, and you regularly encourage them for doing it, they're less likely to do things that require negative consequences."[ix] It's also important to distinguish the child from the behavior. Consequences can only be effective as teaching tools when you communicate that the consequence is the result of behavior, not because the child is "bad." Even though children may not like a consequence, it's important for parents to let them know that they are still safe, loved, and valued. This will ultimately help boost the child's self-esteem and help him or her see that their behavior does not define them.

It's important to consider each situation you find yourself in with your child, take a deep breath, and decide what steps need to be taken to make sure he or she understands how they can do things better in the future. Read on for more tips on how to use consequences as beneficial teaching moments:

***

YOU'VE GOT THIS!

Use contingencies to teach children about completing something before starting something else. Contingencies use 'when' statements to tell children what will happen after they comply with a request. These statements could include, "When you've cleaned up your puzzle, you may get out another toy," or "When you put on your coat and mittens, then you can go outside."

Use choices, especially for strong-willed children that desire more control. Taking the example at the beginning of this section, the parent could tell the daughter, "You may wear your fancy black shoes or your new pink sneakers, but you must wear shoes to go to the movie. Which ones would you like to choose?" Or, in the example of the upset child at the store, a parent could say, "You have so many fun action figures in your bedroom. When we get home, should we play with the green one or the blue one first?" Giving children a bit more control like this can help ease power struggles and can even eliminate NO responses.

Practice proactive strategies in order to promote patience, kindness, listening, cooperation, and helpfulness. When parents can be proactive about promoting positive behavior, instead of just reacting towards negative behavior, they won't find themselves in as many situations to hand out consequences. Help your child wait by singing songs or playing quiet games like "I

Spy." Assist your child with busy work and overwhelming tasks by saying things like, "I'll pick up the books while you pick up the crayons." Use manners when asking your child to get something done, like "Please sit down at the table." These strategies can make many tasks more pleasant and can set a positive tone within your home.

***

"I have so many happy memories - playing at the beach on summer vacations, family ski trips in the winter, singing and dancing, making up games, and being silly. However, there were non-negotiable rules, and both my sister and I knew them and knew the consequences for breaking them. I have memories of us not being allowed to play together if we had been fighting - a natural consequence! At the time, we were unhappy and upset with my mother for separating us, but our tears were short lived. It was my mother's job to set the rules and enforce them, which taught us how to be good, honest, kind, and loyal in the long-run."
– Liz, Early Childhood Director

"My parents balanced really well between being strict and open. We had very specific rules (like curfews, for example) and we were expected to follow them and had consequences if they were broken. But the consequences weren't too strict or overbearing. I

don't remember feeling like punishments lasted very long. I would say my parents were strict but very merciful and loving. I think seeing their disappointment due to my actions, but then seeing their love and mercy guiding their actions, showed me how much they loved me...that has always been very clear. This sense of love has created a really strong relationship with my parents today and a bond we all feel."

- Ginnie, Mother of 3

DIVERSITY AND DISABILITY AWARENESS

Why talking about differences helps children appreciate and respect others throughout their lives

> *"Teach young people early on that in diversity there is beauty and there is strength."*
> – Maya Angelou

It's becoming increasingly important to teach children, even very young children, to appreciate all of the beautifully diverse people that make up our world. When parents can teach children early to value, celebrate, and embrace the diversity of people's appearances, beliefs, physical abilities, cultures, and family structures, they will be open to getting to know others, learn from them, and respect the contributions they make in the world. But how can parents start this process? A wonderful way is to be aware of your own reactions to diversity and to create an environment within the home and family where talking about differences is accepted and valued.

Many times children feel discomfort when speaking to others that are different from them. Much of this could be based on fear, sadness, and nervousness...or from the reactions they see from their parents. Tiffiny Carlson, a writer and quadriplegic from a spinal cord injury, has noticed that parents can sometimes react to people with disabilities with sadness or despair. This causes children to be additionally apprehensive. She states, "Feeling nervous, awkward or afraid around people with disabilities will only make your kids feel exactly the same way." Instead, she states that parents should model acceptance in their interactions for their children: "Respond positively and calmly when encountering a person with a disability and they'll do the same (and hopefully into adulthood too)."[x]

When it comes to diversity, parents should have the same awareness in leading their children in interactions with others. Dr. Christopher J. Metzler, a leading scholar in inclusion studies, states that children are always watching how their parents react to others to gauge how they should respond. He states that parents need to, "...lead by not just saying but also by doing."[xi] When children see that their parents are kind and open to all people, their initial fear and apprehension about encountering those with differences will diminish.

It's also important for families to feel comfortable talking about differences. Children are naturally curious, so they will have questions about why some people look different, eat different foods, speak with an accent, or wear different clothing. Sometimes parents may feel their child's questions are offensive and have an urge to silence them, but this curiosity is actually a great teaching opportunity. Questions show that your child is interested in others, so encourage questions and answer in a way that is age-appropriate. For example, if your child inquires about someone with a different skin tone, simply state, "Just like people have different colored hair and eyes, people also have different colors of skin." If your child asks why someone is using braces to walk, you can say, "For some reason he needs help to walk, so the braces help him move around easier." During these brief conversations, it's also imperative to stop stereotypical, hurtful, or judgmental statements that may come up in your child's speech. If this language happens, immediately (but not harshly) discuss why such words or statements are hurtful and should not be used.

There are many ways to make your child comfortable talking about diversity from an early age. Consider adding these activities, discussions, and materials into your child's everyday experiences:

***

YOU'VE GOT THIS!

Incorporate diversity into dramatic play by offering your child dress-up clothing and play food from different cultures. As children play with the items, start conversations about the people that eat that food or wear those clothes and where they come from in the world.

Use music to introduce your child to different cultures. Find music from different parts of the world online or at your library and talk to your child about different instruments and styles of music from around the globe. This will help children see music is made throughout the world, but there are many special ways that different people create it.

Make sure you're child's toys, books, and activities are not homogenous. Read books that feature characters of different races, backgrounds, family structures, and abilities. Find dolls or action figures of various skin tones and with different abilities. There are many toy manufacturers that are now producing multicultural dolls and play figures and those of varying physical abilities. And studies show that when children play with diverse dolls and play figures, they actually show more empathy and are more comfortable discussing diversity.[xii]

Give your child opportunities to interact with others that are different from him or her, and make sure your child understands that just because another child is different, that is never a reason for rejecting them as a friend.

***

"Be a kind, positive advocate for your child, working with professionals and teachers, keeping in mind you both share the ultimate goal."
- Robin, Special Needs Chairperson

EATING HABITS AND PICKY EATERS

How it is possible to get your children to like
more than noodles and chicken nuggets

Have You Been There? You're trying to have a peaceful dinner, but your son refuses to touch the homemade basil and tomato pizza you've prepared. "It's icky," he says. "There's green stuff on it." He hasn't eaten much all day and you don't want him to go to bed hungry, so you trudge back into the kitchen to make him a peanut butter and jelly sandwich. You wonder if you'll ever be able to get through a meal without a struggle at the dining room table...and if you'll ever be able to stop making emergency PB&Js.

Everyone has a food or two that they don't care for, but this list can grow and grow for young children. If your child dislikes more foods than he or she enjoys, you have a picky eater on your hands. The good news is that picky eating is a stage of life that's perfectly normal for young children and usually doesn't last long. Dr. Sara Schenker, a child nutrition specialist, states that even though navigating a meal with a picky eater can be hectic, "Most children grow out of their fussy eating stage and there is no consequence to health."[xiii] Pediatric dietician Jill Castle, R.D. calls picky eating "a rite of passage" and states that most young children will demonstrate some fussy eating habits at some point in their early childhood years.[xiv]

Even though picky eating is relatively normal, it can be hard for parents trying to feed their families a nutritious meal. It's important for parents to consider the factors that may be contributing to their child's selective eating habits so they can try to implement some solutions. Many kids become picky eaters to exert more control within their own lives or show off their new independence.[xv] Other picky eaters may be experiencing a temporary plateau in growth (which can decrease the appetite) or are just genetically predisposed to not like certain tastes.[xvi]

While most kids grow out of these traits and learn to like many foods, there are many tricks that can help make mealtimes much easier. Read on to learn specific ways to help different types of picky eaters:

***

YOU'VE GOT THIS!

If your child thinks a certain food tastes "icky," try switching up your cooking preparation. For example, instead of roasting a vegetable, try serving it raw. Or if your child scoffs at large chunks of cauliflower, try mashing it up like mashed potatoes. Also, children have more taste buds than adults, so bitter foods can be particularly hard for them to eat. Lemon can counteract the bitterness of many vegetables, so try adding a squeeze of lemon juice or some lemon zest as you cook. It's also beneficial to try serving these foods first, when your child is most hungry, before serving a food your child already enjoys.

If your child "just isn't hungry," consider his or her growth. Children won't be as hungry during a plateau in growth as they are when they're experiencing a growth spurt, so your child's appetite just might be shifting. Remember to have patience at the dinner table. Give your child around 10 minutes with a plate before asking him or her to try at least one bite of each type of food. This "one bite rule" will encourage your child to try everything, but not feel overwhelmed by eating too much. Also, it's important to consider proper serving sizes for your child's age: A serving for a young child is only one tablespoon per year of age - basically, just a few bites of each type of food. If your child sees a mountain of green beans on the plate, he or she might be overwhelmed and not want to eat any at all.

If you're worried your child isn't eating enough nutritious foods, try getting creative with your presentation: Make "ants on a log" to turn celery into a fun snack or arrange salad ingredients into the shape of an alligator on your child's plate. Injecting some fun in plating can make nutritious foods much more enticing. Another fun way to insert more nutrition is to use your kitchen appliances to transform foods: Show your child how to make smoothies in your blender with fresh fruit and yogurt or make juice with your juicer out of various fruits and vegetables (like carrots, apples, greens, oranges, and celery). You can even pour juice into molds for homemade ice pops. Not only will this get kids more involved in the kitchen, but it will also teach them about science (turning solids into liquids and vice versa) and expose them to fun and healthy new flavors.

If your child is indifferent about mealtimes, consider that he or she may simply be exercising control and independence. Involving children more in the cooking process can actually help channel this independence in a helpful way. Invite your child to be in charge of selecting ingredients whenever possible and choose his or her own taco fillings, pizza toppings, or create a customized granola or trail mix. Young children also love using kitchen gadgets, so give your child the responsibility of using a rolling pin for pizza or cookie dough, a plastic squeezer for citrus, or a salad spinner. Kids are mesmerized by these gadgets and have some funny ways of describing what they do. When one of my former teachers was showing her preschool class a veggie peeler, one student said, "Oh, that's the thing that makes food skinny!"

If your child won't try anything new, think about turning snack time into a game. Use an ice cube tray and put one bite of several new foods in each section, then let your child sample them. You could also use a spinning lazy-susan with different foods. Then, let your child spin it and stop it when they see something they want to try. This can make trying new foods less intimidating and actually fun!

If you're concerned about your child's healthy growth and development, talk to your medical professional. While rare, some children who refuse to eat need assistance from a doctor, speech pathologist, or feeding specialist to learn proper chewing and swallowing.

ENCOURAGEMENT VS. PRAISE

Why telling your child "Good job" may not be enough

Have You Been There? Your son wants to show you his drawing of a dinosaur and holds it up proudly. You smile and say, "Good job! Way to go!" He can't wait to show you his next drawing...and the next...and the next. Although you're proud of your son, your enthusiasm decreases with each picture you see. Your son gets a little sad when your excitement about his sixth drawing is not quite the same as it was for his first.

Kittie Butcher of Michigan State University Extension and Janet Pletcher of Lansing Community College state, "When we were raising our children, we were told to 'accentuate the positive.' If our kids behaved well, we were told to accentuate the praise like whipped cream on a latte...Then, experts and some parents started seeing children who thrived on that praise and support to the point where they felt they had failed if they didn't get over-the-top congratulations for everything they did."[xvii] But these researchers say that there is a way for parents and caregivers to support children without making them totally dependent on praise. It involves turning that praise into encouragement.

Praise is very global in nature; it's broad and isn't specific to the child. Phrases like, "Good boy," "Way to go," and "Good job" are examples of praise. But, when parents move beyond statements of praise to statements of encouragement, they foster a child's positive self-image and show the child that they are noticed and appreciated. Encouragement involves the parent offering the child specific feedback that is tailored to a particular situation. Statements like, "You are using so many bright colors on your picture" and "You are being so careful building with those blocks so the tower doesn't fall" are examples of encouragement.

Encouragement is even beneficial if the child is unsuccessful in accomplishing a certain task. For example, parents can still offer encouragement by stating, "You tried opening that jar all by yourself" or "I can see that you're working really hard on your project." When parents use statements of encouragement, they put the focus on the effort and experience rather than on the performance or result. This means that encouragement can be provided in nearly any situation!

By noticing the details of what's happening and using statements of encouragement, you're showing your child that you are paying attention, noticing their experiences, and value their efforts.

***

YOU'VE GOT THIS!

Avoid the Old Standbys - The next time your child says, "Hey, Mom and Dad! Look at me!" resist the urge to simply say "Good job!" or give them a generic "Way to go!" Even though these statements may be your immediate go-to phrases, they don't do much to encourage children.

Use Specific Statements - Instead of using an old standby, take a moment to notice what your child is specifically doing. After you take time to notice this, offer an encouraging comment on one of those details. If you need help, try one of these prompts:

I see that you _____
I like how you _____
I noticed that _____
I appreciate how you _____

***

"My best advice is 'you are the best parent for your child.' As long as your children are healthy, cared for and loved, then you are doing great! Have fun and embrace as much as you can…it goes quickly. It's the little moments that add up to a wonderful childhood."
- Missy, Mother of 3

EXTRACURRICULAR ACTIVITIES

Why less is more in the early childhood years

"So much negativity comes from children growing up too quick...and living up to unrealistic standards." - Lauren, Early Childhood Teacher

There are so many choices when it comes to lessons, classes, and extracurricular activities for young children these days, and it seems like these opportunities are starting earlier and earlier. While it's natural for parents to want their children to try new things, extracurricular activities can often put additional stress on the entire family. Transitioning to and from multiple environments is difficult for young children, not to mention the stress parents can feel when they are driving all over town for these classes and lessons. Professor Steven D. Levitt, who conducts research on parental choices, states, "Being rushed from one event to the other is just not the way most kids want to live their lives..."[xviii]

So often, parents believe that earlier is better and exposing children to extracurricular activities early will boost their performance later in life. But current research actually shows that extracurricular activities are not linked to a child's future achievement or success.[xix] And, many times, a young child's brain and body are simply not ready for these experiences. While so many parents want their child to have opportunities to learn new abilities, extracurriculars can often be overwhelming and stressful (for both the child and the parents) if he or she isn't ready.

There is, however, something parents can do to promote future success for their young child, and it doesn't involve registering for more extracurricular activities: It's good and simple play! I believe Carol, a preschool teacher I worked with for many years, puts it very well: "I think parents need to know that it's ok to let their children just be kids and to make sure to find time for them to just play...I think many parents are caught up with always trying to stay one step ahead of everyone and they tend to over-schedule their child in too many ways!"

The key is to be tuned-in to your child's individual needs. If your child seems overwhelmed, fussy, or extra emotional, take stock of the extracurriculars in his or her life. See if scaling these activities back can create more calm and peace within your child's life. And remember these tips before adding something extra to your child's schedule:

***

YOU'VE GOT THIS!

Preschool is Enough - I believe that if a young child is enrolled in a high-quality, play-based early education program, they do not always need to be involved in additional activities. Preschool programs and playgroups give children opportunities to learn social-emotional skills, play with others, learn from teachers, and explore through play. Because these programs provide children with so much knowledge about the world and help them develop the skills they need to become successful later on in life, they really don't need any extra activities on a consistent basis.

Explore Child-Initiated Interests Carefully - If your child does show a genuine interest in learning something new, it's ok to explore options. But be sure to analyze how adding an activity will impact your family dynamic: Will the activity cut into quality time with your child? Will it cause stress with the travel or expense? Is it at a time that will allow your child to be alert and focused? Try to answer these questions honestly before starting the activity. Then reevaluate if something isn't working. Remember, even if your young child is really interested in learning something new…start slow! For example, if your child is interested in dance, pick one class in one style and try that first. Avoid signing your child up for multiple classes per week of different dance styles, even though you may be excited for him or her to explore that interest.

Introduce New Experiences Carefully - Making transitions to new activities can be stressful for many young children. Try not to make too many transitions too quickly. Just the consistency of a familiar place (like a school or a playgroup) or caregiver can, over time, give children feelings of security. This leads to stable growth and development.

Find Parent-Child Activities - There are many organizations that offer classes and learning opportunities for parents and children to do together. Often these are one-time activities that allow parents and children to spend quality time together while learning something new. These types of activities also allow families to explore different interests without a lengthy commitment of time or resources.

***

Don't get caught up in what other children are doing. Do not feel like your child has to be constantly scheduled. Guide your child in selecting a couple of extracurricular activities that he or she is interested in. Don't choose them just because classmates and friends are doing them. Unstructured free time in a safe environment is so important! Young children have many years ahead of them full of packed schedules and little free time...But I also feel like parents shouldn't allow their child to quit an activity before the session or season is finished. No matter

how hard the sport, music class, dance class, or art class is, encourage your child to continue working at it and find some joy in the challenges of the activity."
- Lyn, Teacher

"My parents were older when I was born (34 and 40). They were extremely hard working and busy all the time, but they were also very loving. When we were little they read a lot to us, they didn't play with us. We grew up in the city so we didn't have a yard. Instead, we rode our tricycles and roller-skated in the hallway. We didn't have a TV either. On weekends we went to the farm where we rode our bikes, ran, played with mud, and swam all day. We learned early to entertain ourselves and we had a blast. We had very few structured activities, yet I don't ever remember being bored. Actually, that was the one word we could never use in our house...and I still never use it!"
- Gabriela, Early Childhood Teacher

"Be a part of your children's activities. Coach their teams, be their scout leader, be a mentor to them. Your children like to know that you care (even though they probably won't admit it). It is very rewarding later in life when they remind you of something you played a role in."
- Maryellen and Russell, Parents of 2

FAMILY TIME

How your interactions now will
impact your child's entire life

> *"Family is not an important thing. It's everything."*
> - Michael J. Fox

In doing research for this project, I asked many early childhood professionals, former students, and current parents of young children about their own childhoods and, specifically, their fondest childhood memories. It didn't surprise me that so many of their responses overwhelmingly centered on their own families. I heard stories about traditions, special vacations, family dinners, and even memories of helping each other around the house. I received the same lovely and simple answer from multiple people when I asked what they most enjoyed doing as a child. Their answer? "Being with my family."

Not only are positive family memories powerful enough to last throughout life, they're also essential in helping children develop essential social, emotional, and academic skills. When families spend quality time together, they form strong bonds that foster trust. Even infants can feel these bonds, which help them feel comfortable and secure within their families.[xx] Quality time also strengthens the entire family unit, making children feel more secure in relying on their family members during times of hardship. And when families are intentional about spending time together, they actually help children learn more about how they respond to the world. Teacher Debra Pachucki states, "Family dynamics shape the way kids think, reason, and problem-solve. A strong, loving family unit that spends quality time together can enhance a young child's academic performance, while decreasing her likelihood of abusing drugs or engaging in other risky behavior as she gets older."[xxi]

Although it's hard to deny that spending quality time together as a family is important, it's not always easy to do in today's world. Many parents are working more, some parents have situations where they do not live with their children 100% of the time, and schedules are becoming more crammed and time-sensitive. All of these circumstances, plus many others, can make quality time hard to come by. But there are simple ways to inject some memory-making fun into the moments you can dedicate to your children:

***

YOU'VE GOT THIS!

Focus on QUALITY - Just because you're spending time in the same physical space as your child does not meant that this is actually quality time. Merriam-Webster defines 'Quality Time' as "time spent giving all of one's attention to someone who is close (such as one's child)."[xxii] Even this dictionary definition points to the importance of parents spending this time with their children. But in order to have quality time, a parent's attention must be undivided with no phones, technology, computers, multitasking, or other activities that take your attention away from your children. Even if this can only be for 10 minutes, children will remember having your eye contact, conversation, and complete attention.

Family Time Doesn't Have to be Expensive - While some people I talked to mentioned family vacations and road trips as their favorite family memories, not all family moments have to cost a lot of money. Simply gathering around the dinner table and asking questions can create laughter and special moments that your children won't forget. Also, don't forget to use the activities you already have on hand like board games or the basketball hoop in your backyard. Gather around the table or go outside and get active. These activities will not only provide opportunities to bond, but will also give your children opportunities to listen, follow directions, take turns, and cooperate.

Eliminate Distractions - Parents often have a hard time 'turning off' their brains and dedicating time solely to their children. Thoughts of rooms to clean, shopping lists to make, laundry to fold, and endless errands that didn't get completed can flood through parents' minds (even though they really want to completely focus on being with their children). Dr. Harley A. Rotbart, M.D. recommends this trick to eliminate these distractions as much as possible: "In the course of a crazy day, imagine your biological parenthood clock wound forward to the time when your children have grown and have left home. Picture their tousled bedrooms as clean and empty. See the backseat of the car vacuumed and without a car seat or crumbs. Playroom shelves neatly stacked with dusty toys. Laundry under control. Then rewind the imaginary clock back to now, and see today's minutes of mayhem for what they are: finite and fleeting."[xxiii] Fast-forwarding your parenting clock is not meant to make you sad, but help you prioritize. Your children won't be young forever, but the memories you make together can certainly last that long.

***

"We had the best birthday parties and we had to invite everyone. To this day, my family likes to go over the top celebrating milestone birthdays in various cities. It's a pretty great tradition."
- Nicole, Attorney

"For younger children, just try to laugh with them every day. Silly things, goofy things, funny things...whatever. Those are the times they will remember and share with their own children."
- Tom, Attorney and Father of 3

"What's most memorable about my childhood is not the time spent away from home (like at Girl Scout meetings, sports, and ballet classes) that I remember fondly, but all the times spent playing at home with my siblings. We spent hours playing make believe games, running races, playing hide and seek, taking picnics to the nearby pond, riding bikes, and eventually playing board games and card games. Family vacations were a HUGE part of my childhood...my parents really stressed the value of family time."
- Sharon, Early Childhood Teacher

"Tell your child you love them, everyday."
- Pat, Principal

FEARS

How a monster in the closet can help you and your
child communicate and solve problems together

> **Have You Been There?** You just tucked in your
> daughter for the night and are ready to relax.
> Suddenly, before you've even stepped out her door
> you hear, "Mom! There's a monster under my bed!"
> You remind her that monsters aren't real and that
> she needs to close her eyes because it's getting
> late. But, less than five minutes later, you hear her
> shout for you again. "The monster is still there...I
> know it!" she says.

Fears are quite common in the early childhood years.
Much of this has to do with children's imaginations and
perceptions of reality. Because they can't always decipher
what's real from what's imaginary, kids can be scared of
things that are very real, but also impossible. [xxiv] While
fears in young children are common, parents should note
that common childhood fears and anxiety disorders are
very different things. If your child's fears are so
overwhelming that they consistently interfere with his or
her daily life, don't hesitate to consult your health care

professional for help.

There are many coping strategies that parents can employ to help their children work through their fearful experiences, but the first step is simply listening. It's easy for parents to dismiss a child's fear (especially if the child is scared of something make-believe), but minimizing the child's feelings can actually make him or her feel more intimidated and overwhelmed.[xxv] If your child is scared, make sure he or she knows that you're there to listen and want to know more about how they're feeling.

Next, remember that the feeling of fear is universal. Everyone feels scared at times and it's important to communicate this to your child. Sometimes parents try to downplay a child's fears by saying, "Oh, don't worry about that." Instead, try phrases that express empathy so the child knows that his or her feelings are valid like, "It can be scary to go to bed by yourself sometimes, can't it?" or "I understand that you're nervous about being with a new babysitter." When you validate your child's feelings, they realize they don't have to navigate their fears alone. Then you can move towards crafting a solution together.

Remember, young children are experiencing the world for the first time, so fears are natural and should be expected. But listening, empathizing, and working with your child to form a solution can help kids navigate these new experiences and empower them to handle these feelings with more confidence.

***

YOU'VE GOT THIS!

Work Together - If your child is scared of something, real or make-believe, work together on a solution to help the child feel better. When children are involved in solving the problem, they gain more courage and confidence over their fears. Here's a personal testimony from my own life: When my own children were 4 and 6 years old, we moved into a new home. The kids were nervous about sleeping in the new house. After I talked with them about their fears, I asked if they had any ideas for how they might not feel so scared. They believed a *Ghostbusters* 'proton pack' would help them feel safe...it was the 80s after all! The children used it to "ZAP" away anything that made them scared about being in the new house, whether it was an unfamiliar noise or something imaginary under the bed. This child-led solution actually helped them cope with their fears and feel much more secure being in a new environment.

Scared of the Dark? - It's common for children to fear the dark, which can make bedtime particularly challenging. In addition to a nightlight, consider offering your child a bedside flashlight. This will provide your child with a tool to investigate his or her bedroom and receive the peace of mind that everything is all right, even when the room is dark.

Specific Fears and Phobias - If your child has a specific fear or phobia, be understanding, but don't cater to the fear. For example, researchers and child psychology professionals recommend that if your child is scared of the ocean, don't deliberately avoid the beach. Provide your child with support to handle the situation, like the "home base" approach. In this circumstance, parents can place a beach towel safely away from the water to use as the "home base." Parents can then go with their child to explore the water, but tell their child they can return to "home base" if they need to before venturing out again.[xxvi]

FINE MOTOR DEVELOPMENT

Why the key to strong years in school
lies in your child's hands...literally!

> *"Fine motor skills are essential to dexterity which is an important thing for life in general - think of how many things we do on a daily basis that require the dexterity of our hands."* - Inez Bayardo

Fine motor development has to do with exercising and strengthening the muscles in a child's hands and fingers. Many simple frustrations that children experience on a daily basis actually revolve around their developing fine motor abilities (like getting dressed, brushing teeth, eating with utensils, or using a pencil). These tasks can be very difficult when children don't get many chances to work out the small muscles in their hands and fingers. But when children do have ample opportunities to practice controlling their fine motor movements, their neural processing networks (which support intellectual progress) are strengthened and stimulated. Additionally, as children use and strengthen these muscles, they become more independent and can complete many tasks faster and with greater accuracy. In fact, research shows that one of the most compelling predictors of future academic success and independence lies in a young child's fine motor abilities.[xxvii]

There are many ways parents can provide young children with opportunities to develop fine motor skills, and most don't involve any special materials. However, it is important that parents understand their child's current stage and start small, gradually working up to more advanced fine motor experiences. And be consistent...practice is key as evidenced by some of my former preschool students: Erin was watching Kiley cut tape and asked, "How do you do that?" Kiley replied: "It takes practice, practice, practice and now I'm good at it!"

Read below for ideas on how to incorporate fine motor development throughout your child's day (and at your child's skill level) with items you may already have around your house.

***

YOU'VE GOT THIS!

Consider Scissors - Scissors are an amazing tool for building fine motor skills. But before giving your child a pair, build this skill by first having your child tear and crumple paper. Then, show him or her how to use child-safe scissors to snip pieces of thick paper just an inch wide or so. Once that is mastered, show him or her how to cut wider strips of paper of various weights. When your child feels comfortable doing that, you can let him or her cut shapes out of paper or pictures from old magazines to make a collage. Just remember to start simply and work up to more complex tasks.

Encourage Pre-Writing Skills - Young children can develop their pre-writing skills by first making scribbles. They might create lines, waves, and large circles. Eventually, you can help your child advance to drawing shapes and letters with either a short pencil or crayon tips (which encourage a proper grasp) or with their fingers in sand, shaving cream, or finger paint. Once they're ready for more formal writing, they can copy and trace letters and words before trying to write them independently. Always encourage children to start their writing at the top of a piece of paper and move from left to right. This will get them used to moving their hands and eyes in the proper direction for both writing and reading.

Break Out the Art Materials - Creating an original work of art with crayons, pencils, markers, glue sticks, stickers, and/or ink stamps gives a child a great creativity boost while helping with fine motor mastery. Using the long side of a crayon to color paper over a leaf, stencil, or other flat object gives kids more sensory feedback as he or she creates their art.

See Toys as Tools for Practice - Many toys have built-in opportunities for fine motor practice; dressing dolls, fitting train track pieces together, and stacking blocks are just a few examples. Puzzles are also great because they involve turning, flipping, and placing small pieces in a specific arrangement.

Get Slimy - Tactile materials like play-dough, slime, putty, and sand allow kids to pinch, roll, poke, sculpt, fold…and work out those hands and fingers!

Help at Home - Think of everyday household activities your child can do to strengthen their hands and fingers like putting a key into a lock, using paperclips, putting magnets on the refrigerator, zipping up a duffle bag, putting coins into a piggy bank, or putting a clip on a bag of pretzels. You can even let your child "clean" certain areas of the house with a spray bottle of water and a rag.

Encourage Self-Care - Urge your child to do self-care routine independently. Getting dressed (and practicing buttoning, zipping, hooking, tying, etc.), brushing hair and teeth, washing hands, and using eating utensils will develop fine motor skills and promote independence. But always be available to provide help until your child has fully mastered these skills.

***

More Fine Motor Activities and Games:
Some of these suggestions involve small items and manipulatives, like beads and marbles. Be aware that these pose choking hazards to babies and young toddlers. Always supervise your children when using these items.

- Have your child pick up and sort a variety of small objects (like blocks, spools, coins, dry beans, cotton balls, buttons, nuts, or bolts) and place them into jars of varying sizes (like cups, mugs, jars, or bowls).
- Have fun stacking blocks and other objects around your home like checkers, buttons, boxes, or drink coasters.
- Give children jars and bottles with lids to let them practice screwing and unscrewing them.
- Encourage your child to place rubber bands or hair elastics around containers of varying widths. Older children can practice stretching a rubber band with their fingers to strengthen them.
- Move a spoonful of small objects or water from one container to another.
- Put small sticks in play-dough and have your child practice pulling them out, and then pushing them back in.
- Find small wind-up toys for your child to play with.
- Challenge your child to see how many clothespins they can clip to the top of a coffee can or cardboard box.
- Use a pile of colorful pom-poms and see if your child can transfer them into a container using tongs.
- Use craft sticks to create letters, numbers, shapes, and other designs.
- Get both of your child's hands involved at the same time with lacing beads of various sizes. Have your child string the beads onto a shoelace (with one end taped so the beads don't slide off) or a pipe cleaner (with one end twisted around one bead so the rest stay on).

- Look for manipulatives (or physical tools for teaching a skill) focused on fine motor development like magnet activity sets, lacing cards, and construction sets. Many are available for reasonable prices at websites like www.orientaltrading.com.

FRIENDSHIPS

How strong friendships in early childhood can impact your child's development and overall wellbeing

> *"Friendship is born at that moment when one person says to one another: 'What! You too? I thought I was the only one.'"* - C.S. Lewis

Recently, I've talked with a lot of adults about their favorite moments from childhood and many standout memories have to do with friendships. One man told me that his early friendships had an incredibly profound impact on his development as a person today. He said, "The relationships I built with others during my childhood continue to enrich my life as an adult." Another woman, who was quite shy as a child, told me that her parents helped her overcome her timid nature and meet other children. "Once I was able to do that," she said, "I loved spending time with my friends."

I can attest to the power of early friendships as well: One of my best friends is from my earliest childhood years, actually from age 2 when we moved in her neighborhood. Her name is Molly and we have been close for over 60 years. I believe that we have maintained this friendship for decades because we bonded as children. There was a connection that deepened as we navigated our lives as we grew older: figuring out childhood and adolescence, growing into adulthood, having families, becoming parents ourselves, facing health issues, and taking care of our aging parents. We have roots that go back to our most formative years, so we have always felt safe and secure being together.

Of course, not all children will have a lifelong friend like I've been lucky enough to have. Things change, people move, and sometimes friends simply grow apart. But building friendships in early childhood is an important skill to learn, even if those friendships don't last for decades. Children can take those skills and then apply them to other friendships that will develop throughout their lives. Dr. Paul Schwartz, an expert in child psychology and behavior, states, "Friendships contribute significantly to the development of social skills, such as being sensitive to another's viewpoints, learning the rules of conversation, and age-appropriate behaviors." He goes on to state that friendships also matter because, "More than half the children referred for emotional behavioral problems have no friends or find difficulty interacting with peers."[xxviii]

Luckily there are many ways that parents can play a significant role in sharing the value of friendship with their children. Parents, when they assist their children in interacting within social situations and problem solving with others, can show their children that early friendships can greatly enrich their lives. Read on to learn more!

***

YOU'VE GOT THIS!

Use play as a tool to promote friendships early. Babies, as soon as they can sit up, can face each other during playtime, just to be aware of each other. As children grow into toddlers and young preschoolers, they can parallel play to get more accustomed to being in the presence of their peers. This means that they can play next to one another, even though they might not interact with or influence each other a lot. But even though you may not think much is happening during these experiences, children are actually learning play behaviors from their peers and are developing more words that they'll use to communicate with their friends in the future.

Talk your child through early interactions with peers. Many times, children can't always express what they're feeling to a new friend because their vocabularies simply aren't that sophisticated yet. But when parents can help their children express themselves and understand a peer, both of the children will become more understanding of the other's emotions. This is called, 'emotional coaching' and can happen when you state something simple to your child like, "He's upset because you took the toy out of his hands," or "She's smiling because she likes painting next to you."[xxix] Using this kind of language to speak about friendships with your child will make a positive difference in his or her developing social competencies.

Show your children that friendships are important by taking the lead and giving children time to spend together. Friendships can't grow if children don't get much time to spend with their peers. If your child isn't enrolled in an early childhood learning program or preschool, look for play groups in your community, different classes for families at your local recreation center, or just get to know the families with children in your neighborhood. For friendships to grow and social skills to develop, parents must play an active role in creating opportunities for their child to interact with others their own age.

Show your children that you want to know their friends and their family. It was always a tradition for my family to host a Christmas party every year for our children's friends and their families. We typically had a house full of 50 or 60 adults and children every year. We wanted to know the parents of our children's friends to open the doors of communication as we raised our children together. We also wanted to know the children better and build a sense of community and friendship. My daughter now continues the tradition with her friends and their families and they affectionately call each other "Framily." Open your homes, have a cookout, or start a regular game night...these traditions and fostering of friendships can last a lifetime.

***

"As much as intellectual growth was a priority in my family, so was social development."
- Irene, Retired Teacher

"My favorite memories from childhood are from the activities I was involved in with my friends like parties and sleepovers...having those friendships was always the most fun to me."
- Missy, Mother of 3

"Although I have no biological sisters, I have my best friend of 64 years who is my sister in every way possible. She is the witness to all of my life, as I am to hers. Before school days, careers, husbands, or children...we have always been together having fun, helping each other to celebrate life's joys, and giving meaning to the sorrows of our lives. I owe this wonderful gift in large part to our parents, both hers and mine. They brought us together when we were babies and throughout our childhood they made it easy for us to be together so that the deep bond between us was established and cultivated. We were inseparable as children, together from dawn to dusk during sleepovers, vacations, camps, summer school, regular days, and holidays. I don't know that our parents intentionally helped us to forge our friendship, but I do know their encouragement and efforts led to something invaluable to my friend and

me. Our lifetime together as real sisters and sharing all aspects of our daily lives has bonded our hearts and souls."

- Molly, Mother of 3 and Grandmother

GROSS MOTOR DEVELOPMENT

How movement improves a child's
health and academic success

> *"We were doing a running-in-place movement activity during large group time today. Craig commented, 'My legs are smoking!'"*
> - Classroom notes from Alice, Retired Preschool Teacher

Gross Motor Development involves exercising the arms, legs, and torso to complete certain movements and skills. When children don't have enough opportunities to move these areas of the body, they can develop problems with energy, endurance, strength, and learning developmentally appropriate skills.[xxx] But when children are able to engage in regular, consistent, and active physical play, they strengthen not just their bodies, but also their minds. In fact, researchers at the University of Illinois found that gross motor activity in young children doesn't just improve overall health, but actually promotes academic progress as well: it enhances memory, attentiveness, self-regulation, the ability to endure the length of a full school day, and overall scholastic achievement throughout childhood.[xxxi]

However, it is important that children learn how to master gross motor skills in an appropriate sequence. There is a certain course of developmental milestones that children must meet before moving to the next step; for example, children must first roll over, then crawl, then walk, then run. Many preschools and childcare centers provide parents with assessments that show the progress their child has made in mastering gross motor skills. This may include how the child handles a ball (that they can throw it with two hands, toss it underhand or overhand, or catch it, etc.). It's necessary for children to master these gross motor skills in an evolving sequence rather than splinter skills where a child could skip over basic foundations for learning.

Because of the physical and cognitive benefits associated with gross motor development, parents should encourage their child to get up and play everyday, but in a way that makes sense for his or her specific developmental stage.

***

YOU'VE GOT THIS!

Focus on Regular, Loosely Structured Play - Encouraging active play is key, but this can be done in an organic, fairly unplanned manner. Start simply, but try to work up to some form of gross motor play each day to build your child's endurance and interest.

Keep Your Child's Developmental Stage in Mind - Remember, gross motor development looks much different for babies than it does for preschoolers:

- **For Babies -** Focus on building muscle strength and gaining control of the limbs. Have fun with tummy time; encourage rolling and grasping with soft toys, and work up to crawling, then walking.
- **For Toddlers -** Toddlers that can walk have more body awareness and body control. This is a great time to introduce large balls that they can practice kicking or tossing. It's also a great time to bring physical activity into everyday play: pretend to walk like a certain animal, have a dance party, catch a ball with two hands, and jump to catch bubbles.
- **For Preschoolers -** These children are practicing mastering balance, speed, coordination, directionality, and understanding positional words (like under, over, beside, in front of, behind, etc.). Games like 'Follow The Leader' and 'Duck Duck Goose' give children opportunities to practice these skills. You can also encourage running by playing tag or chasing bubbles across the lawn. Instead of walking across the floor, challenge your child to skip, gallop, or hop instead. And use your neighborhood playground and equipment specific for your child's age and abilities; this is a great way to encourage children to climb, crawl, swing, and slide.

HOME ROUTINES

Why children need structure to become
confident, self-assured, and independent

Have You Been There? Your son just can't get
moving in the morning. You feel like you have to
remind him about a dozen times to brush his teeth
and get dressed. By the time he's finally ready for
preschool, you scramble to find something he can
eat quickly for breakfast in the car because you're
running so late. In fact, you've been late getting out
the door every morning for a week.

Routines are essential for early growth and
development because they help children feel secure,
engaged, attentive, and prepared to learn.[xxxii] But parents
can often struggle with establishing routines within the
home. This could be because of assumptions made by
adults. Parents know the general routine of each part of
the day, but this knowledge isn't automatic for young
children. It takes a great deal of practice for kids to get the
hang of when they're supposed to do certain things. Adults
may not always realize this process, leading them to
repetitively remind (or even nag) children about what they

need to do. All of this can lead to a good deal of frustration for both parties.

But in my years in the field of early education, I've seen firsthand how consistent routines help children develop a positive self-image and gain autonomy. When adults do the work required to teach children about routines, kids feel safer, more secure, and are more trusting of their environments and caregivers.

If it's been hard to establish a routine, or be consistent with your current one, it may be time to intentionally teach it. Children learn the order and dynamics of routines when they are modeled and repeated by their parents. Practice what you want your child to do and be intentional about showing the steps; don't hesitate to dissect routines into smaller parts. In fact, when parents take the time to break routines down into small steps, children better understand their overall purpose.[xxxiii] For example, parents can break down a child's morning routine into steps like *make the bed, get dressed, eat breakfast, brush teeth*, etc. Parents can even post these steps on a poster board where their child can see them. Little by little, parents can then introduce more routines that promote independence (like getting ready for bed) or contributing to the household (like setting the table or putting away laundry).

Teaching these routines takes time and consistency, but when children finally understand how routines work, they bask in their newfound independence and abilities. Within this process, children also learn about their role in taking care of themselves and others within their family.

***

YOU'VE GOT THIS!

Use Visual Cues – If your child misses a step in a routine, don't feel like you need to provide a verbal reminder. Parents and caregivers can make visual cues so they don't find themselves raising their voices or getting frustrated. Try pantomiming brushing teeth, washing hands, or combing hair…and see how long it takes for your child to remember that step.

Print Photographic Reminders – Take photos of your child doing each step in a routine, then print and post the photos in sequence. This offers the child a step-by-step visual plan of what they need to accomplish. Writing the routine on sticky notes posted around the house works well for older children.

Maintain Flexibility – Not every day is going to be exactly the same, so it's important to be flexible when it comes to your routines. Just as children need to learn consistency, they also need to learn how to handle change. If your routine becomes disrupted, tell your child that you are going to do something different, provide the reason, and assure him or her that you will return to the routine the next day. When you communicate this plan to your child, you're modeling how to remain calm in the face of sudden change.

INTERRUPTING

How focusing on urgency and empathy
can halt persistent interrupting

> *"You need to talk to the plumber, but you can barely hear yourself think above the din of your four-year-old: 'Daddy, Daddy, Daddy!' You put your hand over the phone and ask, 'What do you want?' 'Um,' says your preschooler, who is suddenly decidedly less insistent. 'I saw a bug today.'"* - Susan Spicer

"Mom, Dad...Mom, Dad...MOM, DAD!"

How many times have you been interrupted by your child while you're in the middle of a phone conversation, speaking with your spouse, or just making conversation with the cashier at the grocery store? It can be frustrating, but interruptions mostly occur because young children are often only focused on their own needs. They don't yet realize that adults have needs too. But helping children pay more attention to the needs of others will actually help control constant interruptions.[xxxiv]

Ending the interrupting cycle starts by creating a dialogue with your child before he or she is in a situation to interrupt. Let your child know that you will always be there to take care of his or her needs, but teach when interruptions are appropriate (like when someone is hurt) and when they're unnecessary. Take time to explain and discuss these different situations. Let children know that if something is urgent, you will tend to it right away. But if the situation isn't critical, let your child know that he or she will have to wait for your full attention if you are busy with something else.

Once your child has a better understanding of urgency, you can then start to discuss empathy. Talk to your child about thinking of others, including you. It can be something as simple as saying, "I really need to speak on the phone right now. I will be with you in ten minutes." This also helps your child know what to expect, which may decrease his or her urge to interrupt. Conversations about empathy are also good opportunities to talk about manners. Let your child know that proper manners, like not interrupting unnecessarily and using phrases like "excuse me," are important in developing positive relationships with others, including those within the family.

***

YOU'VE GOT THIS!

Try This 'Tactile Response' Trick – Recently, I have seen an old trick pop up on social media which, in my over

40 years of experience in educating and interacting with young children, has worked quite well. This trick helps children feel heard, even when parents and caregivers can't immediately answer them:

- If your child is repeatedly calling for you, but you are busy or are speaking to someone else, provide a tactile message by placing your hand on your child's shoulder or holding one of his or her hands. This will let your child know that you see them, hear them, and understand that they need you...but that you are not available at that very moment. This contact will serve as a clue for your child to indicate that they are safe and will be tended to soon, but will have to wait until you have completed your other task or conversation.
- Pick a tactile response with your child before trying this trick; something that you both will remember to use. When first attempting it, try to respond fairly quickly so your child can see that this technique will work. Then, over time as you both get used to using this trick, you can lengthen your response time. Just give your child a gentle pat or hand-squeeze to communicate that you're still there and will be with him or her soon.

KINDERGARTEN TRANSITIONS

Why helping your child prepare for kindergarten
sets the stage for a successful school career

> *"The most important day of a person's education is
> the first day of school, not Graduation Day."*
> - Henry Wong

Parents can have many mixed feelings when preparing to send their child to kindergarten. Regardless of whether the child has previously been in a preschool program or at home with a caregiver until this point, children and parents can be nervous, excited, anxious, or scared about entering the world of formalized school for the first time. But there are many things you can do to prepare your family for a successful year in "big school" and beyond!

You may have heard that kindergarten classrooms are more scholastically advanced than they were years ago. While it is true that your child should be able to count, write his or her first name, recognize shapes, and name colors before entering kindergarten, early childhood education professor Ann Barbour states that it is just as important for your child to know how to play well with others, show independence, and problem-solve. She states, "There are many components of kindergarten readiness, most of which are not generally considered to be 'academic'; even though they directly influence how children learn." [xxxv] These areas include motor skills (like opening a lunch box or holding a crayon), cooperating with other children, listening to adults, following directions, using language effectively, paying attention, and being able to handle feeling frustrated or upset. If your child has plenty of practice in honing these skills before kindergarten, it will greatly build his or her confidence and will allow him or her to retain much more information. And when children feel confident in the classroom, that excitement to learn carries over into subsequent years in school.

Regardless of your child's academic or social-emotional readiness, he or she may just be plain nervous to start school. Try some of these tips to ease the apprehension and set the stage for a successful first year...and for years to come!

***

YOU'VE GOT THIS!

Start in the Summer – For children that are especially nervous about transitioning to kindergarten, don't put off these discussions until the week that school starts. Use the summer before kindergarten to talk through your child's new routine and answer his or her questions. Take your child to visit the school's playground and travel the route he or she will take to get there each day. Attend any summer events the school might hold like kindergarten round-up, new family orientation, a meet-the-teacher event, or a supply unpacking night. If necessary, see if your school would allow you to take a tour of the classroom with just your family, so your child has more time to get used to the environment and ultimately feel more at ease when school starts.

Use Play and Books - It may be helpful for your child to use dramatic play to explore his or her feelings about going to school. Role-play different school situations that may come up with your child; use dolls, action figures, stuffed animals, or puppets. You can even play "school" by letting your child be the teacher. Not only does this play get your child engaged in talking about school, it also gives him or her the opportunity to practice the social-emotional skills needed for a successful year. There are also many wonderful picture books that tell stories of young children going to school for the first time. Check these out at your local library and read them with your child throughout the summer.

Tell Them They're Not Alone - Many children may think they're the only ones feeling scared about starting kindergarten and that the rest of the class will be just fine. Let your child know that he or she isn't alone in navigating these nerves. Tell your child how you felt when you had to go to school for the first time and how it ended up being just fine. If you have older children, have them tell the same stories. Above all else, let your child know that many of their classmates are probably feeling anxious too...and that's ok! Let him or her know, "It's normal to feel scared, but once you get to know what kindergarten is like, you'll be able to learn and have lots of fun!"

***

"As parents look at how their child is developing, they can naturally compare this development with other children they know - maybe a friend's child or classmate. But it is important to think about the 'whole child' and not just that one skill the child can or cannot do. One child may be able to identify all the letters of the alphabet and a parent frets their child cannot do the same. But that child who knows all of her letters may struggle socially, with gross motor or fine motor skills, or in some other developmental area. As a teacher, I had several conversations with parents this year about this very topic during parent-teacher conferences. They seemed relieved when I reminded them that each child has different developmental skills they might be working on."

- Lisa, Early Childhood Teacher

LANGUAGE DEVELOPMENT AND PRE-READING SKILLS

How talking more can help your child be ready to read

> *"Language is free. It's a gift that we can give our children anytime and in any place. The only thing that it costs us is our time."*
> - Dr. Debra Jervay Pendergrass

Young children, even before birth, are tuned in to the importance of language. Children can hear and recognize the cadence and rhythm of language prenatally, so providing them with many opportunities to develop language skills is essential as they grow.[xxxvi] Exposure to language, at even the youngest stages of life, is vital in providing children with a firm foundation for future academic success in reading, comprehension, and writing.[xxxvii]

Many experts agree that the key to developing a young child's language and pre-reading skills is to simply speak in their presence...a lot![xxxviii] This means that by just talking to your child about what is happening in your home, what you see at the grocery store, or what's taking place outside your window exponentially grows his or her capacity to develop language. Creating a language-rich environment (by exposing children to conversations, descriptions, and commentary) encourages good communication and literacy competencies that are necessary for kids to become successful readers.

Besides talking, parents should also focus on emphasizing the symphony of sound that surrounds their child's world. Singing, rhyming, reading, and practicing simple finger plays aren't just amusing activities for children; they are actually key components in developing phonological awareness (the ability to hear and identify sounds in spoken words) and auditory skills (which help children process speech, understand phonics, improve their own speech, and acquire reasoning). Both phonological and auditory awareness are important for learning to read and comprehend words.

There are many facets that contribute to a child's developing language and pre-reading skills, but try not to be overwhelmed by these details. Just remember to spend as much time as possible communicating out loud with your child, whether that's through singing, speaking, rhyming, or reading!

***

YOU'VE GOT THIS!

Play with Words – Clap out the syllables of the words you say, tap the syllables in your child's name using a drum or rhythm sticks, or introduce new words with a call-and-response chant. You could also consider teaching your child a new word each morning and see how many times you can use it throughout the day.

Use Books - Reading aloud to children, for as little as a few minutes each day, rapidly increases their brain's capacity for language. Make reading experiences interactive and fun by using silly voices, sound inflections, pointing to words and pictures on the pages, and asking your child questions about the story.

Focus on Rhyme - Sharing nursery rhymes helps children develop a better understanding of our spoken language. Rhymes help kids learn about common sounds and syllables; this assists in future reading and writing. You can also incorporate finger plays (hand movements that correspond with spoken words) into rhyming. Not only are finger plays fun, but they also help young children develop better hand-eye coordination, follow instructions, and remember the words to the rhyme better. Many adults already know the finger play that goes along with *The Itsy-Bitsy Spider*, but there are many more. Search online for other finger plays to enhance more commonly known rhymes.

Incorporate Music and Sound - When children are regularly exposed to music and rhythmic sounds, they will be able to better decipher patterns in spoken language. Sing often, listen to calming music, or even play a "guess-the-sound" game: Make a recording of familiar sounds and let the child guess what they are.

***

"Take the opportunity to exchange ideas about what might happen next before turning the page during a narrative. 'What do you think...? Let's read and find out!' Remember to include nonfiction, poetry, and songs along with the fiction. Don't forget that you are their role model in life and reading, so let children see you enjoying books!"
- Irene, Retired Teacher

Classroom notes from Alice, Retired Preschool Teacher, showing how much language preschool-aged children absorb and how they use it in fun and surprising ways:

"While reading a book to the children the word 'junk yard' came up. After explaining that a junk yard was a place you put things you no longer wanted or were no longer useful, Chelsea said, 'Yes, like the Celebration Army!'"

"As a lead-in to our 'stained glass' apple project, I asked the children if they knew what stained glass was. Brooke replied, 'It's when you leave glass outside and it gets dirty and then you have to wash it.'"

LYING

Why fibs, white lies, and half-truths are normal
and can even signal positive development

Have You Been There? You're sitting down at the dining room table to look through some mail when you notice the rug underneath your feet is wet. You look under the table and see a red, child-sized cup tipped over with a little bit of white milk still resting inside. When you call your daughter into the room, you ask, "Did you spill your milk and not clean it up?" She looks you straight in the eyes and says, "I didn't do it." When you remind her that no one else is home and that you certainly didn't spill the milk, she states matter-of-factly, "It was Max." Max is her imaginary friend.

All parents want their children to be honest, and most begin telling their children that lying is wrong at a very young age. But research shows that children often start telling lies as early as age 2.[xxxix] While this can cause some parents to panic, they need to consider that this behavior is actually very normal and can even be a sign of positive growth and healthy development. In fact, lying is a sign that children are becoming more mature and aware of the world around them. Early childhood researcher Lara Warmelink states, "In order to lie, children have to understand that other people have their own beliefs and thoughts that are not the same as theirs," and that awareness is actually a very positive development in a child's life.[xl]

Even though lying isn't uncommon, parents still want their children to understand the importance of honesty. So instead of getting upset when a child lies, use the situation as an opportunity to teach the truth. Because young children have fairly short attention spans, lectures on lying won't often work. Instead, when your child tells a lie, just spend a minute or two talking about how you value honesty in all situations. Don't dwell on the lie, just briefly discuss it, and then let it go until you run into another teachable moment. If you're consistent with this pattern, your child will feel more comfortable coming to you with the truth as he or she grows.

Knowing the types of lies kids tell at certain stages of development can help you navigate the various untruths you may hear from your own children. Read on to find out the types of lies kids tell at different ages and how you can encourage honesty in each circumstance.

***

Toddlers and Self-Effacing Lies – A child's first fibs are often the ones that get them out of trouble or allow them to gain a reward. If you notice these types of lies from your own child, try to focus more on the situation than the lie. For example, if you notice that your child has broken one of his or her toys state, "Look, that toy is broken," instead of "Why did you break that toy?" The first statement points out a situation, while the second presents an accusation. Often, when very young children are accused, they will lie.[xli] But by simply paying attention to the situation, you open the door for a child to discuss what happened honestly.

Preschoolers and Tall Tales – Children reaching preschool age often make up tall tales and fantastical situations and insist that they are true. Parents should explain to these children that, even though these situations may seem real, they aren't actually what is happening. Point out the differences between fantasy and reality, not to shame your child, but to communicate that swapping the truth for pretend isn't appropriate. But tell your child that it's perfectly acceptable for him or her to make up stories for fun, as long as they tell you and others that these tales are imaginary.

School-Aged Children and Lies to Avoid Disappointment – Children as young as 5 might start telling lies to avoid parental disappointment. For example, if a child gets a bad grade on a test, he or she might lie and say that the test was cancelled. These lies can happen because the child is scared of facing the disappointment of his or her parents. This can cause lots of internal turmoil within a young child, so instead of immediately punishing the child for lying, find out what caused him or her to lie in the first place. Understand that lies like this may happen because the child is trying to show sensitivity to your feelings, which is also an important developmental milestone.[xlii]

NEGOTIATING

Why young children are not prepared to play
"Let's Make a Deal" with their parents

> *"Negotiating techniques do not work all that well with kids, because in the middle of a negotiation, they will say something completely unrelated such as, 'You know what? I have a belly button!' and completely throw you off guard."* - Bo Bennett

Parents today can often feel conflicted when it comes to setting boundaries and saying 'no' to young children. Many want to parent with logic, so they attempt to reason with their children to get them to see things from a more mature perspective. Many times, parents take care to thoroughly explain the reasons why their children need to do things like wear a coat in cold weather or wash their hands before they eat. But when parents only use these types of explanations to tell children what they need to do, they run the risk of negotiating matters that should be quite matter-of-fact. They also hand over a lot of authority to the child that he or she is not prepared to accept.

Even though many young children can seem like

master negotiators (often convincing their parents to let them spend an extra 10 minutes on the playground or push back their bedtime), their brains are not actually developed enough to make wise decisions that are in their own best interest. Neil Swidey of The Boston Globe states that when children are regularly given "logical" explanations from parents, they become trained to negotiate too early. He warns, "...no matter how articulate a 4-year-old is, his brain is not built for adult concepts like abstract reasoning and delayed gratification."[xliii]

This means that many times parents need to set solid, non-negotiable boundaries for their children. These boundaries are not just beneficial for a young child's developing brain, but they are actually what children need to feel more comfortable and safe. When children are put in positions to negotiate, they get a convoluted perspective of who is in charge. This can lead them to not feel as secure as they should. As Swidey states, "Deep down, most kids take comfort in knowing that, at the end of the day, someone else - someone far more qualified - is in charge."[xliv]

If you find it hard to set boundaries without entering into some sort of negotiation with your child, read on for ways to cut down on the back-and-forth:

***

YOU'VE GOT THIS!

Use Statements, Not Questions – Many times, negotiations can be avoided completely when parents state their request instead of asking their child a question. For example, if it's time to go to bed and the parent asks, "Are you ready to go upstairs?" the child gets an opportunity to say no and then negotiate a later bedtime. But by stating, "It's time to go upstairs and get into bed," parents aren't opening the door for a potential deal. They are simply stating what needs to happen. Bottom line: Do not ask your child a question if you're wanting them to complete a non-negotiable action.

Make Schedules to Provide Structure – When children have predictable schedules and routines, they won't feel the need to negotiate as much. If a child doesn't want to put away his or her toys, use the schedule to explain that the toys must get picked up so that lunch, which is the next activity, can occur. Schedules offer young children a greater sense of order and sequence; they are less likely to resist moving on from something if they know what's coming next.

Offer Limited Choices – Even though questions should not be used for non-negotiable actions, you can ask your child to make a choice surrounding that action. This gives the child a greater sense of control within the boundary. For example, if it's time to get ready for bed, ask, "Would you like to brush your teeth or put on your pajamas first?"

If your child is having trouble, you can offer assistance as one of his or her choices, like, "Would you like to put on your pajamas by yourself or would you like me to help you?"

Safety First – Remember, safety rules are non-negotiable. Holding a parent's hand in a parking lot or putting on a seat belt are actions that young children must do, no questions asked. I always used the word "Danger" when my children were young so they understood that the action was non-negotiable and that I meant it! The word "No" is often said too many times, and too loosely, so children may test you when you say it. "Danger" communicates the seriousness of the situation.

Remember You're Not a "Mean Parent" - Just because you set firm boundaries doesn't mean that you have to be stern with your child all the time. Standing by non-negotiable actions could elicit some tears from your little one, but you can still offer him or her lots of love and understanding. When you simply say things like, "I understand that you're upset," and "I know it's hard," you show your child that you're not a cold and uncaring dictator, but a loving parent that will help him or her come to a better understanding of what needs to be done.

PARENTING IN THE FAST LANE

How to have special moments with
your child in the midst of your busy life

> **Have You Been There?** From driving your children to school and activities, going to work, and making quick stops in between to pick up a gallon of milk here and some dry cleaning there, you feel like you're constantly on the go. But even when you're home, you still feel like you're in the fast lane: laundry needs to be folded, dinner needs to be made, and then...your phone alerts you to several emails and notifications that you just can't put off. These days, you feel lucky to even have a conversation with your children, yet alone sit down and play with them. Can you make life slow down?

Families are constantly in the fast lane these days. There are so many places to be and so much to get done on a daily basis that it can seem overwhelming, especially if you feel like you're not spending enough quality time with your children. Of course, parents can't completely ignore their to-do lists. But while not everyone can hire a driver or private chef to help cross some things off the list, families can learn to find joy and opportunities for connection as they tackle their busy lives. Even though you probably don't love running errands or dusting the living room, you can actually use these experiences to interact with your children each day.

Instead of thinking that you have to complete certain tasks before you can focus on your child, try bringing your child into these experiences. Psychologist Nicole Beurkens believes that any number of household tasks, chores, and errands can be transformed into memory-making opportunities for children and parents. She states, "You're spending time doing things like cooking, taking the dog for a walk and doing laundry, so why not include your child? This not only allows for valuable one-to-one time to talk and to connect, but it also teaches them important life skills."[xlv] Many times these tasks also give parents and children opportunities to have more meaningful conversations, like when a child is close to your eye-level while riding in a shopping cart or when he or she is in the backseat of the car without the radio on or a device to play with. When parents can find ways to incorporate time spent with their children and their daily responsibilities, they'll find that they're making the most of their time and perhaps not feel quite as overwhelmed.

But it's also essential that parents limit their own distractions to make the most of the time they do have with their children. This means putting down cell phones, resisting the urge to have a "perfect" and spotless home, and avoiding checking social media. Instead, put your full attention into the precious moments you do have to spend with your child. When you eliminate distractions, electronics, and perfectionism, it will actually make the time you spend together feel much longer and more meaningful.

Need some ideas to find more time to connect with your children in the midst of your fast-paced life? Try these:

***

YOU'VE GOT THIS!

Think of All the Things Your Child CAN Do – Instead of trying to rush through your chores, think of how your child can participate. Even very young children can help you put away groceries on a low shelf in the refrigerator, add clothes to the washing machine, or put cherry tomatoes into a salad for dinner. When you focus on the things your child can do to help cross things off your to-do list, you'll create more time to spend with each other. You'll also teach your children how they can be helpful to others within the home.

Use Car Time Wisely – Don't be frustrated that you're stuck in traffic, but think of the amazing potential you have to make memories with your child in the car. Turn off the radio and talk about your child's day. Play car games (like counting all the red cars you see on the road) or make up silly stories together. If you like listening to music, make it songs that you and your child can sing together. Try singing in crazy voices or even making up your own song. You can also find children's audiobooks to listen to together in the car; just be sure to make time to talk about the story and ask your child questions about what they liked about it.

Make Mornings Memorable – If you're finding it hard to sneak in special moments with your child, don't overlook the time you have together in the morning. Try your best to prepare as much as you can the night before and then get up 10 or 20 minutes earlier in the morning. This could be just the right amount of time to snuggle, color a picture, or read a book together before you have to leave the house. All of these extra minutes in the morning can really add up to significant extra time together.

***

"Laughter is still an overwhelming memory when I think back on my childhood. I definitely have some hilarious memories from road trips, trivia in the car, and making inside jokes we still recall 25 years later. My favorite memories are of all of us laughing together. As an adult, I am happy to say that tradition is going strong. Laughter isn't just 'the best medicine,' it's like a daily vitamin you need to survive!"
- **Athena, Young Professional**

"A parent should prepare their children for the road rather than preparing the road for their children. Easy advice, but really hard to do. I probably continue to do the latter. It is all about control and when to know when it is time to yield this control. It probably cheats them of developing confidence but certainly cheats them autonomy they are entitled to."
-Evans, EdD, Child Clinical Psychologist

PARENTING STYLES

Why thinking about how you parent, and how your parents parented, impacts your children today

> *"Parenting is the hardest thing I have ever done. I tried to find the balance between the strict, traditional Chinese way I was raised, which I think can be too harsh, and what I see as a tendency in the West to be too permissive and indulgent. If I could do it all again, I would, with some adjustments."* – Amy Chua

Psychology scholars have identified four major styles of parenting: authoritative, authoritarian, permissive, and neglectful. These styles impact the environment in which a child grows and develops. Understanding parenting styles is critical, especially since research has now revealed that a child's traits are the result of both genetics and his or her environment.[xlvi]

- **Authoritative parenting** stresses high expectations, but still focuses on being responsive to a child's needs. This style creates a healthy environment and fosters the bond between the child and the adult.

- **Authoritarian parenting** (or strict parenting) focuses on demands, but not necessarily responsiveness. These parents focus most on directives and punishment without leaving room for discussion.
- **Permissive parenting** is overly responsive, but lacks in demands. These types of parents are very warm towards their children, but establish few (if any) rules. This can result in children that lack self-control or self-discipline.
- **Neglectful parenting** is harmful to a child's development and overall safety. Neglectful parents are uninvolved, unresponsive, and/or indifferent towards their child's needs and interests. These parents often need assistance so that they can learn how to establish a healthy relationship with their children.

Remember, parents always love their children, but don't always like their behavior. Parenting styles determine how parents naturally react to this behavior. Everyone has innate responses for handling situations with their children; some are laid back, others are strict, and some are expectation-driven. Likewise, everyone has responses that don't come as naturally. For example, maybe you show your child plenty of love, but find it hard to discipline. Perhaps you can see some of these divergences as you look back on your own childhood. I've recently asked some current parents of young children about this and I've heard, "Growing up, there wasn't enough consistency in how I was parented. I think that's something I always keep in mind as my children develop and grow," and "Having divorced parents, I felt I had two separate parenting styles - one was the fun party house where I got to experience the joys of life. The other was the grounded and disciplined house. Both were full of love but very different."

Because of these variances in natural responses, it's important for parents to be mindful of their natural style and try to create a better balance of love with structure. From decades of research, child psychology professionals have found that the authoritative parenting style produces the most positive outcomes in children, so trying to move towards this style fosters an environment with more communication, boundaries (which children both need and want), and love inside your home.[xlvii]

Establishing a more authoritative parenting style takes time and practice. The key is that parents always ask themselves how they can improve their natural parenting style to become more balanced in care and expectations. It's an ongoing quest for improvement that doesn't take place overnight. In fact, my message to my adult children is to be present, be available to listen, and be willing to learn about your children. I tell them I did the best I could, learned from my mistakes and my successes, and want them to do better with their own children.

***

Think Back to Your Own Childhood – Understanding the different parenting styles is extremely important, not just in determining your own natural style, but in understanding how you were parented yourself. Think back to when you were a child and ask yourself these questions:

- *What was the parenting style of my own parents?*
- *Did my home environment balance nurture with clear expectations?*
- *Is my natural parenting style the same as my parents? If not, can I move towards a style that creates more balance with my own kids?*

Look at the Whole Parenting Picture – Once you've answered these questions, consider the bigger picture: What did you witness your parents doing? How does that influence your own parenting, if at all? Once you take your own childhood into consideration, you can more accurately understand your natural parenting style and how to create a more authoritative and balanced environment within your own home.

***

"I would say that my parents were balanced between being strict in some ways as well as permissive in others. Overall, these approaches were balanced

appropriately 90% of the time. Certainly I could have been forced out of my comfort zone a few times here and there, but overall I would say they nailed it. I do not have children at this time, however I cannot see how my upbringing would not influence how I raise them when the time comes. There are certainly ways in which I would mimic how my parents raised me...and ways I would do the complete opposite. I would teach my children how to treat and interact with others as I was taught..."

- Justin, Production Manager for ABC

"I think parents need to know to take each day one step at a time; don't sweat the small stuff. Everyone will have an opinion on how you should raise your child and you have to follow your heart and do what you feel is best for them."

- Ashley, Nutritional Case Manager and Mother of 1 Son

"Parenthood is a marathon, not a sprint. This is hard to remember when you are running the daily race that is parenting young children, but if you keep the long-term goal in mind, it puts these bumps in perspective and gives you inspiration to keep running!"

- Liz, Early Childhood Director

PLAY IS ESSENTIAL

Why play, above all else, is the ultimate learning tool

> *"I am in preschool. I am not built to sit still, keep my hands to myself, take turns, be patient, stand in line, or keep quiet all of the time. I need motion, novelty, adventure, and to engage the world with my whole body. Let me play! Trust me, I'm learning!"*

Scholars, researchers, and education professionals have consistently agreed that play is a powerful tool in helping children learn. Researchers from the National Association for the Education of Young Children (NAEYC) state, "...learning occurs best when children are mentally active (not passive), engaged (not distracted), socially interactive (with peers or adults), and are building meaningful connections to their lives."[xlviii] All of this best occurs when children are given the time, space, and encouragement to play.

Children are truly special and their innocence resonates in every wide-eyed discovery of the world around them. Every play experience is also a learning experience that enhances this discovery. To see this in action, simply watch and listen to your children at play. You will find out so much about what they already know, need to learn, and think about the world around them.

Many parents worry that their child isn't participating in enough formal learning experiences. But, for the early childhood stages, the learning that takes place through play is the most vital. In addition to helping children acquire practical knowledge, play gives children more tools to become compassionate, caring, and creative.[xlix]

But children should not be left to their own devices to learn through play. They need the adults in their lives to help organize and participate in this play as well. Read on for tips on how to promote learning through play within your own home.

***

YOU'VE GOT THIS!

Let the Child Direct Dramatic Play – Allow your child to have control over their dramatic play experiences, but still be a willing participant in this play. Think of your child as the director and think of yourself as one of the actors. Enter into the conversation, ask questions, or play a role in your child's dramatic play...just follow your child's lead. This will help keep children engaged in play experiences so more learning can happen.

Provide Open-Ended Materials – Open-ended materials

are those that kids can use in many different ways. These include play-dough, water, paint, sand, and blocks (or other building toys). The beauty of open-ended materials is that, even if you give a group of children the same materials to work with, each child will ultimately create something unique and individual. Since there are so many options for children to use open-ended materials, their creativity and critical thinking abilities are exercised: They execute plans, make decisions about how to use the materials, experiment, make predictions, and develop their own unique ideas. Children can also learn about science, engineering, design, and math as they stack blocks, build LEGO towns, or create structures from Magna-Tiles. Parents can encourage more learning and exploration by asking kids questions and providing ideas. You could ask your child, "Do you think you could build a tower using all the blocks?" or "What might happen if you mix these paint colors together?" As you ask these questions, you're not just supporting your child's creativity, but also his or her developing language skills.

Create Sensory Bins – If you've ever Googled or searched Pinterest for something like 'Learning Activities for Young Children,' you've probably seen ideas for sensory bins. Sensory bins are basically large containers filled with materials and objects to create a tactile environment for engaging a child's senses. All you need is a container (something durable and large enough for children to dig in), some type of filler (pom-poms, water, water beads, snow, kinetic sand, shredded paper, etc.), and some simple household objects (like scoops, spoons, funnels, or measuring cups). Simply put the filler in the container and give kids the freedom to touch, scoop, dig, and explore in the bin. Children love sensory bins because they stimulate the senses, allow for creative exploration, and provide new ways for them to investigate.

Experiment with New Ways to Create – Children sometimes like straightforward activities with predictable outcomes, but they also really love experimentation, unpredictability, and getting a bit messy. Don't be afraid to engage in play with your child that explores new ways to create. Try new art materials, make something out of found or recycled materials, or use an old item in a new way. For example, instead of drawing or coloring on plain construction paper, encourage your child to create a picture on a sheet of newspaper, from a page in a catalog, or even using a scrap piece of fabric. Or, instead of using paintbrushes, see what kind of art your child can create by dipping their hands and feet in some paint instead. Small alterations like this can turn everyday play into exciting new ways to design and explore.

Don't Forget to Get Outside – Playing outside opens many doors for creative and imaginative play, so get outside whenever possible. Additionally, many of a child's developmental achievements can be effectively learned, practiced, and mastered through outdoor play. For example, picking leaves, grass, and flowers improves fine-motor skills; running and climbing through a playground structure develops gross-motor abilities; and simply exploring an outdoor environment teaches children more about science and the natural world. Significant amounts of learning can happen when play is taken outdoors.

***

Classroom notes from Alice, Retired Preschool Teacher, showing how simple play can teach children more about the world:

"Craig and Conor were playing with the race cars. They were having a conversation on how fast they should go. Craig said, 'We can't have them go too fast because we'll get a speeding ticket and that won't be good.'"

"David was playing with Tucker the turtle puppet today. He was sitting on the floor with Tucker on his hand looking at him for a long time. Then he looked at me and asked, 'How do you make Tucker think?'"

QUESTIONS

How to turn a child's never-ending questions
into meaningful teaching moments

> *"Why is the sky blue? Where did the dinosaurs go?*
> *Why can't I stay up late? How do planes stay up in*
> *the sky? Where do babies come from? Why do*
> *children ask so many questions?"* - Rynette R.
> Kjesbo

A variety of questions can spew out of children's mouths, seemingly, from nowhere. In fact, once verbal, young children typically ask about 228 questions per day![1] Parents can often feel inundated and overwhelmed by these constant (and sometimes quite random) questions, but it's important to remember that asking questions is a major component in how young children learn. They are generally curious about the world because so much of what they see and experience is new and fascinating. Questions naturally stem from this curiosity.

But asking questions is also an important part of a young child's development. When a child asks questions, he or she is effectively practicing verbal communication skills. Through questions, children learn more about conducting conversations and listening to others. They may also use questions to let adults know that they're feeling uncomfortable, anxious, or scared about something. For example, a child that asks "Why do I have to sleep with all the lights off?" may be developing a fear of the dark.

Although question asking is a beneficial and positive behavior, it can still be a bit agitating for parents when the questions are non-stop. But remember that these are valuable learning moments, so try your best to have patience and see questions as an opportunity to teach your child. Try not to ignore your child's requests for information and provide answers to the best of your ability. And if you don't know the answer to a burning question, just say so...then tell your child, "Maybe we could find out the answer together." This shows your child that learning takes place not just in the early years, but also throughout life!

If you're feeling overwhelmed, have confidence in the fact that your child is coming to you for answers. Keep the lines of communication open to show your child that he or she can always ask you for help. This will make it easier for your child to share things with you in the future.

Try these tips for making questions more of an interactive and family-focused experience:

***

Make a Question Jar – Get a large jar and cut several small strips of paper to put next to it. Then, when your child asks you a question that you don't have adequate time to answer in that moment, write the question down on one of the strips and place it in the jar. Then, designate a special time each day to pull out a question and answer it for your child. Make sure to do this when you have ample time and won't be distracted, just in case the question requires research or a lengthy explanation.

Answer Questions at Mealtime – A young child's questions can make wonderful conversation starters for the entire family. Around the dinner table, encourage your child to ask questions about something they're curious about. Different family members can help answer the questions and offer new insights that you may not have considered.

Use a Timer – If your child's questions become relentless, set a timer for 5 or 10 minutes and designate this as "Question Time." During this time, allow your child to ask any number of questions about whatever he or she wants, but when the timer goes off they need to take a break. This is particularly helpful for children that have rapid-fire questions that they want answered immediately.

"What I've Learned Watching My Daughter Parent:

1) How impatient I was as a parent!

2) It's a good thing I was her PARENT and NOT her friend because it helped her develop by teaching her consistency and discipline (versus being her buddy).

3) Don't interfere...they are HER kids!

4) I'm impressed with her determination and confidence to be a phenomenal mom all the time.

5) I'm amazed by her energy level, which she uses to make her children's days as joyful and educational as possible.

6) It's important to give your kids the chance they deserve to show what THEY can do!"

- Bill, Father and Grandfather

READING ALOUD

Why there is no legitimate substitute for a good ol' book

Have You Been There? You've heard that reading to your child is important, but your daughter just isn't interested in books. Every time you pull a book from the shelf, she says "No! I want to play a game on the tablet instead!" You've tried many different books, but nothing seems to hold her interest.

Jim Trelease, author of <u>The Read-Aloud Handbook</u>, references a 1983 U.S. Department of Education report that found, "The single most important activity for building the knowledge required for eventual success in reading is reading aloud to children."[li] But the benefits don't just stop at helping children become successful readers. Research shows that reading aloud to children actually increases their brain's capacity for language, enhances their auditory comprehension skills, expands their vocabulary, helps them develop coping strategies, increases their general world knowledge, strengthens their relationships with parents and caregivers, and builds their self-esteem.[lii]

There simply is no substitute for a cozy lap or a parent's arms; no CD, video, tablet, or computer can duplicate the calming, soothing, reassuring, and educational experience of sharing a book together. That's why it's important for parents to read to their children each day no matter what. With a little imagination and persistence, both parents and children will find that sitting down with a book creates unique and special experiences (even if the same book is read over and over again). By using different visual responses, sound inflections, and asking questions during a reading experience, adults can greatly foster their child's curiosity, imagination, and overall interest in books. When adults engage with children through stories and get excited about reading with them, they are communicating very important messages: books are important, reading together is fun, and time spent with books is time well spent.

***

YOU'VE GOT THIS!

Read at Least One Book Each Day – Take time everyday to read aloud to your child...it's just that simple! At least one book per day produces immeasurable results in the life of your child and creates amazing memories for your family. If your child is resisting reading during the day, try right before bedtime so there won't be the option of picking a different activity. Then try working up to more books throughout the day.

Use Supplemental Activities – To enhance your child's interest in curling up with a good story, inject some supplemental activities into your reading experiences to make them more interactive:

- Use puppets or stuffed animals to act out the story.
- In a dark room, shine a flashlight on a puppet as a child manipulates it. It will not only amaze your kids, but will also help them learn about shadows and sizes.
- Read through a story once, then read it again slowly and encourage your child to act it out as you read.
- Use books with repetitive words or phrases, encouraging your child to recite those words or phrases with you.
- Solicit input from your child on what to read next. Find out your child's interests and go to the library to find books on that particular topic.

Notice How Your Child Remembers Details – Extending your reading experiences through activities and supplemental activities aren't just pleasant ways for you to spend time with your child, but can really help him or her remember specific details from a story and get them thinking. For example, I read a book about 'The Gingerbread Man' to my grandson and then we made gingerbread cookies. After cutting gingerbread people out of dough, I noticed that he had built a wall on the end of the cookie sheet. When I asked him why he said, "So they don't run away when we open the oven. I want to eat them!"

SCREEN OVERUSE

Why too much screen time can impact your child's
language skills, relationships, and overall health

> *"Whether you are a parent or not, carving out time to turn off your devices, to disconnect from the wired world and engage with the real people who are all around you, is one of the best gifts you can give yourself and the people you love."*
> - Alan Brown

While technology is making our world much more advanced and connected than ever before, there are still significant concerns among teachers, physicians, researchers, and parents about how these advances (specifically screen technology) impact a young child's developing mind and body. Psychologist Madeleine Portwood says that, specifically, many children's language and social skills aren't developing as rapidly in the early childhood years because of their increased access to screens. She states, "For example, a child learns to develop conversational skills – you ask a question and somebody answers and then you develop it. If you don't have these opportunities because you're keyed into an iPad or computer game...children's communication skills become limited, and that affects social relationships."[liii] And since games and videos present children with a multitude of sounds, images, and colors all at once, children often have trouble concentrating after exposure to that stimulus for a prolonged period of time. If children don't get sufficient "practice" at learning how to verbally communicate or focus on off-screen tasks, their skills in cooperating, asking questions, listening, and following directions may severely lack as they grow older, which will not only impact their relationships, but also their years in school.

A child's growing body can also suffer from too much access to screens. This overuse in children has been linked to health concerns including significant headaches, eye issues, and sleep problems from the "blue light" emitted by phones and tablets. Screens have also been linked to the rising obesity rates among young people because children simply aren't engaging in enough active play and movement.[liv] Many physicians urge parents to consider their child's sensitive makeup before providing him or her with a device. Dr. Robert Block, Past President of the American Academy of Pediatrics, states, "Children, however, are not little adults and are disproportionately impacted by all environmental exposures, including cell phone radiation. In fact, according to the International Agency for the Research on Cancer, when used by children, the average RF (radiofrequency) energy deposition is two times higher in the brain and 10 times higher in the bone marrow of the skull, compared with mobile phone use by adults."[lv] A child's sensitive young body simply isn't built to withstand prolonged screen use.

But it's also important for parents to take a hard look at how children are utilizing technology within the family structure. Parents can often think it's acceptable for a young child to spend a couple of hours with an iPad in his or her lap because they're playing an "educational" game, but the type of education that the iPad provides isn't necessarily the type of learning that's most needed at that stage of development. [lvi] What is needed, many early childhood professionals agree, are opportunities for children and adults to cultivate meaningful conversations, learn how to ask and answer questions, and play through being active and using the imagination. Further, children at this stage are craving time and attention from their parents...something that a screen will never be able to recreate. As Dr. Portwood states, "But, however exciting a game is – video, iPad or whatever – a child will always prefer to have their parents' time."[lvii]

Are you finding it hard to tear your young child away from screens? Read on for ideas on how to manage screen time and decrease your child's risk for developing screen-related health or developmental problems:

***

YOU'VE GOT THIS!

Distinguish Screen Time from Play Time - Play is the fundamental and best learning tool for young children. That said, screens are now being considered by many parents to be toys for "play time." Instead of thinking of screens as toys, think of them as a separate opportunity all together that is limited to a certain amount of time each day (which most professionals recommend as not more than one hour per day). When screen time is limited and separated from other types of play, parents show their children the importance of setting boundaries, using their imaginations, and being active.

Get Involved - While limiting screen time is important, it's just as important to get involved with your child's activities in front of a screen. Nicole Dreiske, Executive Director of the International Children's Media Center, recommends that parents talk with their children about the videos they watch and the games they play just like they would talk about the characters, plotlines, and conflicts in a book.[lviii] When there is parent engagement like this, a child's vocabulary and literacy skills can actually increase as a result of this purposeful screen time. And talking together about movies, TV, Internet, and electronic games is a natural extension of positive family communications.

Make Mealtimes Screen-Free - Eliminate screens from the meal table, including when you're out at a restaurant. While it can be tempting to pack the iPads to have some adult conversation while out to eat, doing this doesn't teach your children about manners, properly engaging in conversation, interacting with others (like the restaurant staff), or being mindful of other patrons. Use meals to focus on listening, sharing, and cultivating good discussions.

Set a Good Example - It will be harder for a child to disengage from screens if his or her parents are consistently looking down at their own phones or tablets. Remember, your children learn from your example: If they see you spending a lot of time with your face in front of a screen, they'll also want to use technology at the same time. Try your best to save your time on social media for your lunch break, during naptime, or after your children have gone to bed.

***

"Today, I am most concerned about my children's health, both physical and mental. I worry they will be somewhat detached and lack important empathy and skills needed for a productive and happy life because they have been exposed to so many different influences that were not a concern when I was growing up (like the media, online access, video games, and violence). I think these things have influenced my children, even though I always try to be vigilant."
- Heidi, Mother of 2

SELF-ESTEEM

How parents are essential in helping children feel
confident, capable, and valued

> *"Parents need to fill a child's bucket of self-esteem so high that the rest of the world can't poke enough holes to drain it dry."* - Alvin Price

Self-esteem isn't just important in helping a young child feel valued and accepted. Building a child's self-esteem is also essential in helping him or her face the many new experiences that are going to come along as they grow. When young children possess the self-esteem to feel confident about these experiences and try new things, they're more likely to give their best effort, feel proud of their accomplishments, handle making mistakes, and persevere in the midst of setbacks. And one of the major factors in building a young child's self-esteem, according to Meredith Ross and Allison Hall of Vanderbilt University, is through positive early interactions with parents. They state that parents have a tremendous impact on their child's understanding of self-worth and help a child come to "form his or her own concept of self..."[lix]

Working towards boosting a young child's self-esteem can actually start soon after birth when parents show infants plenty of love, protection, and care. As babies grow into toddlers, parents can build self-esteem by letting them try things on their own and assert some independence while also paying attention to their accomplishments. Then, as these children grow into preschoolers, parents can promote self-esteem by giving them plenty of opportunities to try new things, learn about the world through play, and feel secure and understood.

There are some amazingly simple things parents can do to immeasurably impact their young child's self-esteem. Try these with your young child:

***

YOU'VE GOT THIS!

Create a Secure Home Environment - Ross and Hall state that a calm, loving, warm household better allows children to feel comfortable expressing themselves. [ix] When parents create a home environment that makes their children feel safe to open up, better communication will flow resulting in more opportunities for positive and uplifting conversations.

Teach, Show, and Allow Mistakes - Your child needs to be able to rely on you to help him or her learn new skills at each stage of life. Be intentional about teaching your children, first through showing them how to do something new, helping them do it, letting them try by themselves (even if they make mistakes), and being there to encourage them until they've mastered the action. Once your child "gets it," remind him or her of all the steps it took; this will help him or her feel proud of the accomplishment and recognize the hard work and perseverance it took to get there.

Use an 'I Can' Can - This is a fun visual way to remind your child of all the things he or she can do and should feel proud about. Find a coffee can or tall Pringles can and some craft sticks. Each time your child learns to do a new task independently (like getting dressed, putting on shoes, or riding a tricycle) write that task on one of the craft sticks and drop it in the can. In time, children will want you to read off all the activities in the can. Then they can count the number of sticks representing all the activities they can do. This will reinforce messages that your child is smart, capable, and can tackle all kinds of new challenges.

Be Conscious of Your Own Self-Talk - In order for your children to start believing in themselves, they need to see an adult "walk the walk." If you constantly talk down to yourself, don't be surprised if your child starts doing the same. Ross and Hall remind parents, "the higher self-esteem you have for yourself, the more likely your child is to have a high self-esteem as well."[lxi] Because of this, practice positive self-speech, then pass this onto your children. Try something like, "I'm really proud of this dinner

I made. It tastes good," then ask your child, "What is something you did today that made you proud?"

***

"I'd like our children to be confident and secure in who they are as individuals and not let anything shake that."
- Jackie, Mother of 2

"My goal for my own two children is that they would be kind, resilient, and happy no matter what they choose to do in life. I feel that if they possess those attributes then success will come."
- Heather, Early Childhood Teacher

"Showing your child that you trust them to navigate a situation without you there adds so much to their growth as an independent and capable human being."
- Sharon, Early Childhood Teacher

SEPARATION ANXIETY

Why showing confidence can help your child
overcome fears of being away from you

Have You Been There? Your son is starting
preschool and for the first two days, he's sobbed
as soon as you take him to the classroom door.
After a long and tearful goodbye, you stick
around and peek through the windows for as long
as you can. Then, at work, you call and email the
school's director multiple times to see how he's
doing. Even though the director has reassured
you, and has even emailed you a picture of your
son happily playing, you can't shake the worry
and the guilt.

Young children, on the first day of school or first time with
a new babysitter, may certainly cry when you leave. In fact,
he or she may cry each time for several days or even several
weeks. It's a painful process, not just for children, but
certainly for parents too. It can be hard for parents to put their
trust into others to meet their child's needs. And, of course,
parents don't want their children to feel like they've been
abandoned. These feelings can cause many parents to shed

just as many tears as their children.

Even though your child's sadness can make you feel awful, don't panic or feel like a bad parent. The truth is, your child's tears don't mean that he or she doesn't like his new school or babysitter – in fact, he or she may soon grow to love this new experience. The problem lies in the fact that your child doesn't want to do something new without you...and this is actually a positive sign that your child feels a strong and healthy attachment and bond with you. Also, he or she has come to trust you for every need; it's only natural that he or she wants you close to navigate a brand new experience.

Even though going through the transition to a new caregiver can be hard, it is important to help your child grow, learn how to cope, and become more independent. In order to accomplish this in a way that makes your child feel secure, it's most essential for parents to remain confident and composed on the outside (even if they're crying on the inside). Research shows that when parents stay calm and show confidence during these situations, children feel secure in the new situation faster.[lxii] Even though you may be sad, trust the teacher or caregiver to handle the situation in a loving and nurturing way. Good preschool teachers and childcare providers have successfully dealt with many similar situations in the past, so have faith in their expertise.

Try these tips to give you and your child more peace of mind and feel more confident when transitioning into a new care or school situation:

***

YOU'VE GOT THIS!

Use concepts children understand when talking about what will happen with a new caregiver. Always reassure your child that your separation is only temporary and that you will always come back. Remember that children don't yet have a concrete sense of time, so they won't understand it if you say, "I'll be back in a couple or hours," or "I'll pick you up at noon." But if you say, "I'll be here right after you're done eating lunch," your child will better understand what to expect.

Focus on your child during goodbyes. Even though seeing your child cry can be difficult, it's important that you give him or her your full attention before you leave. Look into your child's eyes, show confidence, avoid displaying your sad emotions, and use your voice to reassure your child that he or she will be safe and will even have fun. What worked best in my school was when children were left by a confident parent who gave a hug and a kiss and trusted the teachers to help the child calm down and have fun.

Make goodbyes brief, even though you may want to linger just to make sure your child is ok. This only makes the transition more difficult. After you tell your child you're leaving...leave. For children that have a particularly difficult time and cannot adjust or self-sooth, I recommend that parents implement the 'leave quick and come back soon' strategy. If you can, start with some shorter time transitions, like 30 minutes, then build up to an hour and eventually longer. I've seen this strategy work with many families in my preschool whose children eventually became very excited about coming into the classroom.

Let your child bring 'special items' to feel more comfortable. It was my preference as a preschool director to allow children to bring one 'special item' (like a stuffed animal) to school. We let them keep it with them for about 10 minutes and then they had to put it in their individual mailboxes in the classroom. Then, the child could go check on the 'special item' by giving it a squeeze throughout the day before going back to play. This little piece of home helped ease some worry for a lot of students.

Provide caregivers with family photos. Many preschools encourage parents to bring in family photos to display around the classroom. Just seeing a family photo can help a child who is missing his or her parents. Another strategy I've seen is for parents to make a photo key ring with their house key on it and put it in their child's backpack. Caregivers can then tell the child something like, "Mommy and Daddy are working, but they will come back to get you because you have the key to the house!"

Remember, it won't last forever. Separation anxiety is a normal occurrence that is only temporary. Until the phase passes, focus on reassuring your child that you will always come back and celebrate your child's perseverance as he or she becomes more comfortable at school or with a new care provider. And kids that can have a hard time separating can eventually become very self-assured and confident, as evidenced by one of my former preschool students. I recently heard this from his mom:

"Your school and your guiding principles and advice were a beacon to me as a new mother and I was so grateful because I fully trusted you. I recall a day I was exhausted by my son Gregory...It was your advice to keep him in school (but to wait in the parking lot for a bit in case he didn't calm) that kept me sane and more importantly, helped him to have early school success and the confidence to 'stick it out' even when circumstances are difficult. Today Gregory is confident and strong in the face of the adversity he has faced so far. He doesn't give up and was taught, through this one example, that he can persevere."

SHARING

Why forcing your child to share doesn't teach generosity

> *"The waiting is the hardest part."* – Tom Petty

If you've been around two or more children at the same time, you know that sharing doesn't happen easily. If a child's sights are set on a certain toy, he or she certainly doesn't want to wait for it or offer it up to someone else. In fact, Dr. Laura Markham states that arguments amongst children most often stem from them both wanting the same toy: "After all, your son hasn't looked at that toy in over a year, but as soon as his little brother unearths it, he can't live without it in his sole possession."[lxiii]

While this arguing can be tiresome, it can also be hard because parents want their children to think of others, be fair, and be generous. This can lead many parents to get involved and initiate 'forced sharing.' This happens when a child gets upset waiting for their turn with a toy, so the parent decides that the child with the toy must pass it on.

But Dr. Markham states that the idea of "forced sharing" may actually do more harm than good in the long run. She states that even though this method may seem quick, easy, and fair, "it reinforces competition between siblings, dis-empowers both children, and teaches children that if they fuss, they get their way."[lxiv] Instead, she suggests that adults focus more on the good feelings associated with giving and generosity. Forcing children to share leaves them feeling resentful, not generous. But when a decision to share is initiated by the child, sometimes called a 'self-regulated turn,' they'll feel good about sharing and will be more likely to share again in the future.[lxv] This happens when the child with the toy decides how long he or she needs it, and then gives it to the other child when they're done. Even though this process can sometimes take much longer than 'forced sharing,' it teaches the child with the toy that he or she won't be forced to give something up without a warning and teaches the child that's waiting about patience and gratitude.

Moving from an atmosphere of 'forced sharing' to 'self-regulated sharing' isn't easy at first for children or adults. But as kids get the hang of it, you'll see them communicating more with each other, asking for turns, offering toys to each other, and being more generous overall. Read on to learn more about how to implement 'self-regulated sharing' in your home:

***

Focus on Taking Turns - A good way to start is by letting your children know that each of them will get a turn with a toy, even though they may have to wait. To the child using the toy first, state, "When you're done playing with that, will you please give it to your sister? Thank you!" Then work on helping your children use words to initiate the sharing themselves.

Avoid Taking Something Away From One Child to Give it to Another - When adults snatch things out of their child's hands to give it to another child, it's actually sending a complicated message; it teaches children to take from others, grab what they want, and be more protective over their possessions. All of this makes children less likely to share because they want to hold on to everything they can, for fear it will be taken away. Instead, simply remind your child, "When you're done with that toy, your brother would like a turn." It may take several reminders when first starting this process, but children will pick it up when it's used consistently.

Teach Your Child How to Wait - It's hard for a young child to wait for a toy. Minutes can sometimes feel like hours and patience can run thin. But you can help your child wait effectively by redirecting him or her to a different activity, providing a listening ear, or just giving a hug and kiss. Sometimes children just need suggestions to remember that there are many other opportunities for fun.

You can even put together some special activities that are only available when a child is waiting, like a small box of mystery toys. Also, remind your child that the sharing rules apply both ways: Once the toy is in his or her hands, there is no time limit! This can help make the waiting a bit easier.

SHYNESS

How to help children gain confidence in interacting with their peers

Have You Been There? You and your daughter have joined a playgroup and, when you go to the first meeting, your daughter won't leave your side. All of the children are very friendly and many come and ask your daughter to play, but she only shakes her head and plays alone right next to you. You hope it's just a case of the jitters and that she'll engage more next time. But for the next two weeks, she does exactly the same thing. She resists joining other children, even though they play games and use toys your daughter loves. You're beginning to worry that she's going to have a hard time making friends and you really don't want her to feel alone.

Some children have a naturally shy, slow-to-warm up temperament that can cause them discomfort in new situations or surroundings. But new or unexpected circumstances can cause even the most outgoing children to experience bouts of shyness.[lxvi] While it's natural for parents to want their children to feel secure and confident around potential new friends and within new experiences, many children simply need more time and intentional practice to handle these transitions.

Rona Renner, nurse and parent educator, states that comfort and time are the essentials children need when they're hesitant about a new situation or setting. She states, "Comfort is the keyword here. Once they are comfortable, they will talk as much as anyone else. They will play as much as anyone else. But they need that time. Don't push your child." She also points out that shyness presents values; many times young children show shyness because they are simply very observant or cautious, which are very important traits that parents should commend.[lxvii]

Instead of worrying about your child's apprehensions, focus on communicating ways that he or she can have fun learning about others. Often, children feel uncomfortable with peers because they are afraid of other children rejecting them, not liking them, or being judged. Child psychologist Carol Dweck recommends that parents teach their children how to focus on others in social situations, which redirects the child's focus away from his or her own discomfort: "You should tell your child that being in social situations is a way to have fun. It's a way to learn about other people. Ask them questions...Tell them to learn new things in these social situations so that the focus won't be on being judged, it will be on learning."[lxviii] Re-framing social interactions in this way can take some pressure off and allow children to release some self-consciousness.

While you can't change your child's personality, you can create opportunities to help your child feel more comfortable as they navigate their new and ever-expanding world. Try these techniques with your child:

***

YOU'VE GOT THIS!

Teach Children How to Meet Someone - Practice social interactions that happen upon first meeting a peer, like smiling, maintaining eye contact, and making self-introductions. It may sound strange to think of intentionally teaching your child to smile or look someone in the eye, but the more you practice these skills, the easier it will be for your child to feel comfortable with new people in new settings. Role-play by pretending to be a new friend; encourage your child to introduce him or herself by saying, "Hi, my name is…" You can also remind your child to "Look at the color in a friend's eyes when you speak" and "Smile, because that tells other children that you're friendly and that you want to play." Practice and play with these situations, especially leading up to a social event.

Go Slow - Don't feel like your child is going to sit on the sidelines forever if he or she doesn't want to jump in and play with other children right away. Allow him or her to sit for a little while and observe the group without pushing for immediate interaction. If there are a lot of children in the group, you can encourage your child to find just one other child to play with to ease into interacting with the entire group. Let your child know that if a another child asks to play before he or she is ready, a polite response would be to smile and say, "Thanks, but I'm not ready yet." Little by little, with more observation and gentle integration into the group, your child will overcome his or her reluctance to participate.

Use Everyday Interactions to Practice - When children have opportunities to interact with others in the presence of a parent, they will feel more confident in social situations with other children. Encourage your child to order his or her own meal at a restaurant, take books to the check-out desk at the library, or take the receipt from the cashier at the store. These interactions with unfamiliar (but safe) individuals will give your child a chance to practice smiling, making eye contact, and using good manners...essential skills that can help them feel more confident and capable of making new friends.

***

"As a child, I had to learn to overcome shyness in meeting other children my age. Once I was able to do that, I loved spending time with friends."
- Yvonne, Young Professional

SIBLING RELATIONSHIPS

How fostering connections early helps siblings feel safe and supported throughout childhood and into the future

> *"Siblings: children of the same parents, each of whom is perfectly normal...until they get together."*
> - Sam Levenson

Sibling relationships are incredibly important in developing a positive and strong family dynamic. It's important that, as soon as a new child comes into the family, parents help facilitate a positive bond between the baby and the other children in the household. This can be something as simple as giving older siblings a chance to interact with their new brother or sister. Dr. Laura Markham states, "Whenever possible, snuggle up with both your infant and your older child, so those feelings of big love they feel on your lap get transferred toward each other...Laughter and physical contact stimulate bonding hormones like oxytocin and reduce stress hormones, so every time you get your children laughing or snuggling together, you strengthen their positive bond."[lxix] When you create opportunities for connection between all your children, you're showing them the importance of a strong sibling relationship that can carry on throughout their childhoods and beyond.

But sibling relationships aren't always so rosy. Anna Goldfarb of the New York Times states, "Siblings are often the only people with whom we have lifelong relationships. For many people that means a built-in best friend for life. But deep, lifetime connections like that can be... messy at times."[lxx] That means that even close siblings will fight, debate each other, and experience rivalries every once in a while. Children may start to tease, insult, or show aggression towards a sibling for a number of reasons: they may need more attention from a parent, they could feel some competition with their brother or sister, they might be reacting to a change within the household (like marital strife or financial stress), or perhaps they simply haven't been taught effective skills to solve problems yet. It's important for parents to analyze these possibilities and try to understand the underlying issues surrounding the behavior. Ask questions, not about the conflict, but about how your child is feeling and what they might need. Once the child opens up about his or her emotions, talk about more positive ways to meet those needs besides picking a fight with a sibling.

Parents should also consider that sibling disagreements could actually be beneficial for a child's development. When siblings bicker and argue, this can be a great opportunity to learn about navigating power struggles, negotiations, compromise, and coming up with solutions to problems. When you can encourage your children to work out their differences, and tell them that you can help them if they need it, you'll find that they will get over their disagreements quicker and they may even become less frequent.

Overall, make it a goal to communicate to your children that your home should feel like a safe space for everyone that lives there. A positive home environment can certainly facilitate strong bonds and lasting memories for all of your children. As someone recently told me, "What was most memorable about my childhood was the camaraderie between myself and fellow siblings. Whether it was playing with each other outside...or whether it was doing chores and working with our father, we we're always doing it together. Those times will always be special to me."

Here are some more specific messages you can communicate to create more sibling harmony inside your home:

***

YOU'VE GOT THIS!

Remember That You Will Always Be Family - When your children are fighting, let them know that their disagreements don't define their relationship or their place within the family. Remind your children that, even though they may not like how their sibling is behaving, they still love them. Use statements like, "Even though your brother is bothering you, we are still a family and we still love each other. So let's see what we can do to solve this problem."

Avoid Comparisons - All children are different. It's important for parents to recognize and celebrate the uniqueness of each of their children and avoid comparing one against the other. When parents imply (either directly or subtlety) that one child is better than the other, an atmosphere of jealousy and negativity will form between the siblings.

Teach the Importance of Words - Harsh words can cut quite deep, so when children sling insults at one another, it can hurt badly. Remind children that, even when they're mad, they may not use unkind or negative words to hurt someone else. Research shows that for every negative comment a child hears, they need at least five positive comments to cancel it out.[lxxi]

Provide Older Children with Sibling Responsibilities - If a new baby is coming into the home, facilitate a positive sibling relationship early by giving your older child ways to help. Perhaps he or she can be in charge of getting the diapers or wipes before a change or keeping the baby entertained with a toy while you prepare a bottle. This not only strengthens the overall sibling relationship, but also shows your older child that you honor his or her contributions to the family.

Use Props to Teach Problem-Solving - Consider using cue cards to give your child a visual reminder of problem solving skills they can employ with a sibling. You can make these by pasting photos or drawing on index cards. Make cards for taking turns, waiting, using words to ask for something, sharing, giving a hug, or asking an adult for help.

Redirect When Necessary - Sometimes siblings simply need some space from one another. In these times, stay calm and suggest that your children participate in separate activities for the time being. Calmly help each child find something to do independently until the dust settles. Maintaining a calm attitude during your redirection will help your children understand that they can also maintain calm when they're feeling frustrated by a sibling conflict. They may even redirect themselves without your assistance the next time.

***

"As a parent, I was sure that each of our three children accepted the importance of others around them, including their siblings, extended family, and friends."
- Irene, Retired Teacher

SOCIAL-EMOTIONAL DEVELOPMENT

Why teaching children about emotions
contributes to overall development

> *"Emotional learning is not a quick or easy lesson. Many adults never master it. But practice makes better. The more practice young children get, the better they will be able to express their emotions and control their behavior."* - Heather Shumaker

In her book, <u>Me, You, Us: Social-Emotional Learning in Preschool</u>, Anne S. Epstein states that social-emotional development is directly linked to a child's future success.[lxxii] Social-emotional development has to do with a child's social competence, how he or she is able to self-regulate, and how he or she understands personal feelings and the feelings of others. These skills are linked to so many proficiencies that children need to be successful in the future, from forming friendships at school to navigating future relationships to working well with others when they become adults. In fact, research now shows that when children develop social-emotional competence, they also progress in their cognitive and academic abilities.[lxxiii]

There are many facets that contribute to helping children develop essential social-emotional skills. These include (but are not limited to) helping children understand a range of emotions and feelings, gaining knowledge of norms and customs, developing self-control, and becoming empathetic to others. While children aren't born with these skills, they do possess the capacity to develop them when adults are there to guide and support them. In fact, some of the best practices to help children learn these skills are what many parents do already: taking time to bond and taking time to play.

The importance of creating strong bonds and secure attachments early cannot be overstated. When parents are intentional about creating these bonds, children feel safe, loved, and are better able to understand social interactions early. These children also come to trust their parents, and as they grow they will look to these adults to model appropriate social behaviors and responses. Further, play is one of the best ways for young children to learn more about their own emotions and the emotions of others. Play helps children become more resilient, develop relationships with peers, solve problems with others, manage stress, prioritize, and learn more about their place within social structures and within the world.[lxxiv]

Even though undertaking the task of teaching your child social-emotional skills can seem overwhelming, remember that children learn best through play and experience. Prioritize spending time with your child to help him or her advance in social-emotional development. There are also many ways parents can support this learning within the home. Try some of the activities listed here to help you be intentional about teaching these essential life- and learning-skills:

***

YOU'VE GOT THIS!

Pretend - Play scenarios are a wonderful stage to let children explore their emotions and engage with others. As you play with your child, use different scenarios to pretend to be different people feeling different things. Use story starters like, "It was my first day of school and I felt…" or "My baby brother broke my LEGO tower…" You can act out the situations with dolls, action figures, or stuffed animals too. After the pretend play, discuss times in real life when your child may have felt sad, happy, worried, etc.

Understand Your Child's Temperament - Your child may be hesitant to engage with peers or other adults simply based on his or her temperament. He or she may be slow to warm up to others or anxious when entering a new social situation, and that's ok. Be there to support your child in navigating these new experiences, talk about them, and let your child know that you will always be there to provide help.

Make a 'Feelings Board' - Many schools are now incorporating these boards in their classrooms, but they are also extremely beneficial for the home. You can draw faces expressing different emotions, cut out pictures of faces from magazines, or take photos of family members showcasing different expressions. Compile all of these images on a chalkboard, whiteboard, or poster board, then ask your child to point to the face that best matches his or her mood. This gives a child a visual key to let you know how he or she is feeling. You can then ask questions about that emotion, why the child might be feeling that way, and what might help if they are feeling a difficult emotion. This assists the child in becoming more expressive by allowing them to move beyond simply saying, "I'm mad," to verbalizing emotions in more detail. As you do this daily, encourage your child to use more sophisticated vocabulary in their descriptions, like *nervous, frustrated, excited, frightened*, etc.

Talk About Feelings Regularly - Make emotional-talk a part of your child's everyday experience. For example, have one meal a day where everyone in the family expresses a feeling or emotion and why they're experiencing it. When your family makes these conversations a regular part of the day, it will be much easier for your child to talk about his or her own feelings and recognize the feelings of others.

***

"I want to be sure to guard the little hearts of today's children from the chaos of the world. As I continue to grow myself, my understanding is not that you can necessarily guard them, but better equip them on how to deal with the harshness of this world...and, better yet, give them the keys to be successful!"
- Katie, Mother of 2

SUPERHERO PLAY

Why playing like Super Man and Wonder Woman
encourages pro-social behaviors

> *"There is a superhero inside all of us, we just need the courage to put on the cape." - Unknown*

Zoom! Swoosh! Bam!

These are the sounds that might come from your child as he or she engages in superhero play. But saving stuffed animals from villains and wearing a towel as a cape aren't just fun activities for children. Research actually shows that superhero play is incredibly beneficial for a child's creative, social, and emotional development. Dr. J. Alison Bryant, a scholar and play researcher, states, "Superheroes offer lessons in values that kids actually grasp...The more kids act out pro-social roles using those models, the more likely they are to keep doing so."[lxxv]

These lessons include helping others, feeling brave, and having self-control. When children engage in superhero play, they are practicing positive social behaviors; they gain confidence, feel that they can solve problems, have a desire to help others, and show kindness. Adults can encourage these positive social interactions by showing children that they can be superheroes by sharing, helping a friend who is sad, or using kind words.

Remember, superhero play doesn't always have to involve your child running or jumping through your home. He or she can use toy hero figures with blocks, in a sensory bin, or in a sandbox. As your child plays, ask questions about what the superhero is doing or offer your child a scenario to expand their play. This will enhance their social and emotional understanding and bolster their imaginations...as they save the city from impending doom!

***

YOU'VE GOT THIS!

Point Out Good Guys vs. Bad Guys - Children don't necessarily distinguish real people from fictional characters. It's helpful to point out a superhero's good characteristics (like kindness and helpfulness) versus a villain's unsavory characteristics (like selfishness and greed).

Differentiate Rough and Tumble Play from Aggression - Sometimes superhero play can be quite active, so it's important to teach children the difference between rough and tumble play and aggression. Falling over, gently wrestling, and hitting without hurting can be fun, but it can quickly turn aggressive if a child feels threatened or humiliated. Teach kids that aggressive behavior, like real hitting, isn't acceptable and means it's time to take a break.

Ask What a Superhero Would Do - When conflicts arise, ask your child, "How would a superhero handle this problem?" By asking your child to think like a superhero, you are putting him or her in the mindset of being brave, kind, and courageous. This can ultimately help them implement positive conflict resolution strategies in their own lives.

What Happens When Superhero Play Becomes Superhero Obsession? – Superhero play can become fanatical if your child: a) Won't take off his or her costume to go to school or go to the store; b) "Dominates" play time at preschool by "forcing" others to join in play that always features him or her as the superhero; or c) Is so focused on the superhero that every drawing, game, discussion, and meal somehow features that character. Rest assured that this stage should pass in about a year. In the meantime, set limits on costumes being worn only at home during playtime or on a visit to a friend's house. Remind your child that, at play, he or she may speak and dress like the superhero, but must use his or her own voice and clothing during meal times and family time. If the child can't self-regulate his or her emotions to stop aggressive actions, remove the child from the play and divert his or her attention to another time when the child can be a happy, kind, helpful hero.

TEMPERAMENTS
OF CHILDREN

Why understanding your child's personality
can make you a more proactive parent

Have You Been There? You and a friend have spent a lovely afternoon at the park with your preschool-aged children. But now it's time to go. Your son kicks the sand, screams, and throws himself on the ground because he does not want to leave. But your friend's son calmly takes his mother's hand and walks with her to their car. Your friend and her son have already left the parking lot as you're still trying to pick up your son and carry him to the car. You wonder what you are doing wrong and why your child won't cooperate but your friend's son does.

Every child is born with a unique way of responding to the world. These innate tendencies are called *temperament* and play a major role in how your child's distinct personality will form. There are three distinct temperament categories: *easy, slow-to-warm up, and difficult.* [lxxvi] Children with an easy temperament are characterized by being particularly flexible. Their rhythms are generally positive and adaptable and they don't get frustrated frequently or easily. They can feel emotional, but may not show these emotions with much expression. Children that possess a slow-to-warm up (or shy) temperament adapt to change slowly and can be uncomfortable with new experiences. They may cling to a parent and feel reluctant to join a group, and their negative moods are often expressed slowly with more sadness than anger. Children with a difficult temperament are more fiery and feisty and may experience difficulties with change. Many times these children resist or adapt very reluctantly to new experiences. These children may be disagreeable and have intense reactions when angry or frustrated.[lxxvii]

While these categories are distinct, remember that they are neither good nor bad. Children don't choose or create a temperament; they are simply born with one. Temperament categories are not set up to make parents feel that their child is better or worse than another. Rather, they are structured to help parents understand how their child responds to various circumstances. And when parents know more about their child's specific temperament, they can learn ways to be more proactive in their parenting. They can help their child respond to challenges and changes more if they understand how the child is wired to respond naturally. Understanding temperaments can also help parents see their role in guiding their child to be successful. Many times, parents believe they're doing something wrong when their child has a hard time adapting to change or a new experience.

But most of the time, the child's inborn temperament determines his or her responses, not a certain parental strategy or misstep. When parents come to understand this, they can take some pressure off themselves, become more effective, and focus on strategies tailored for their child.

Can you identify your child's temperament? Read below for more specific strategies on what your child may need from you based on this temperament:

***

YOU'VE GOT THIS!

Tips for Easy Temperaments - Parents may think, if they have a child with an easy temperament, that they don't need to employ strategies to help their child adapt. However, since these children tend to be generally pleasant and not overly emotional, they may not verbalize their need for more interaction with you. Parents should still make an effort to provide lots of quality time and attention, even if the child doesn't ask for it. Because young children are still growing, developing, and learning about how to interact within the world, they still need focused attention from their parents...even if they don't request it.

Tips for Slow-to-Warm Up Temperaments - Because these children can have a hard time getting used to new people and situations, parents should be sure to introduce these experiences slowly. For example, when attending a new preschool for the first time, make several visits before the child's official first day so he or she can understand what to expect in the classroom. Because these children need extra time to feel comfortable, don't put pressure on them to be extroverted. This can make a child feel like his or her natural tendencies are wrong. What these children need from you is patience and a willingness to take things slowly.

Tips for Difficult Temperaments - Routine and structure are important for all young children, but are extremely vital for children with difficult temperaments. These children don't like to be surprised by sudden change, so maintaining a predictable schedule and talking a lot about changes or new situations before they happen are essential. You can also practice different ways of behaving in challenging situations before they occur. This could take place in playtime moments; have a tea party or play "school" together and practice sharing, trading, using kind words, and taking turns. It's also important for parents to pay attention to stressful stimuli in the home (like too much media, loud or violent television, or shouting among family members) and eliminate it to keep the home more peaceful. This can prevent overstimulation and also help the child calm down when he or she gets upset. And, as often as possible, find ways to notice your child's positive behavior and voice your appreciation when the child shows a willingness to adapt.

THE POWER OF 'NO'

Why it's not only ok to tell your children NO,
but why they actually need to hear it

> *"A society that is determined on protecting children from ever feeling uncomfortable seems to do more harm than good in that it makes them unprepared for the adversity that life has ahead."*
> - Justin, Production Manager for ABC

Parents are facing many pressures today that they weren't in years past. More demanding work environments, divorce, or just the everyday stresses of maintaining the home, bank account, and multiple schedules can lead many parents to feel bad about not spending enough quality time with their children. This can give parents intense feelings of guilt, which can cause some unintended but serious consequences. Author David Walsh, Ph.D. states, "When we are with our kids, we want them to be happy and have positive feelings about the time they spend with us, so we end up doing things they will like, and we're reluctant to say 'no.'"[lxxviii] But this reluctance to utter that little word can actually result in children becoming more impatient, self-interested, and materialistic. It can also lead children, in a world already becoming more obsessed with instant gratification, to believe that they can always get what they want when they want it. But when parents can understand that saying 'no' to their children is actually good for them, it can make the practice a bit easier.

Just how is saying 'no' to children good for them? First, it allows children to experience, and then work through, feelings of upset and disappointment. If children don't have many opportunities to feel let down, they won't learn about how to have resilience, perseverance, or solve problems. In this way, 'no' actually builds a child's self-esteem and independence. Next, 'no' shapes a young child's work ethic. Sometimes, parents resist asking young children to pick up, make their beds, or learn various household tasks because they don't want to spend the little time they have together bickering or listening to the child's resistance. But when children have responsibilities outside of simply making themselves happy, they will quickly learn that life is about more than just one's self. Saying something like, "No, you may not play until your bed is made," to your young child isn't unreasonable. It's actually an impactful way to teach the child that he or she can be helpful, do something for others, and contribute to the overall well being of the entire family. This builds up a child's work ethic early, which will play a major factor as he or she grows into adulthood.

Think about this as well: Children need to hear 'no' from you so they know how to say 'no' to others in the future. As children mature, they will face pressures of all kinds. Of course parents want their children to know how to resist risky behaviors and not give in to others. If these children have had strong parental role models who were able to stand firm and say 'no' to them, they will feel more comfortable resisting pressure themselves.

It isn't always easy to say 'no', but it is essential to build important life skills. Here are some ways to make 'no' a little bit easier:

***

YOU'VE GOT THIS!

Erase Entitlement - If you find it hard to deny your children of everything they want when they want it, remember that this can create a sense of entitlement. To help erase this, communicate limits early. Let children know that you work hard to make money for your family, but it must first go towards the family's needs (like shelter, food, clothing, medicine, etc.). Let your child know that, if he or she wants something extra, they can use birthday money or can do more around the house to earn some money, but you will not be buying that item now. While this may take some time for your child to get used to, you're helping to erase entitlement by letting your child see the realistic side of spending and earning money...which is a valuable lesson that can carry on throughout the child's entire life.

Walk the Walk - In order to teach children about delaying instant gratification and practicing self-control, parents will have to evaluate their own behaviors as well. Have conversations with your kids about the things you might want to buy, but need to save up for first. For example, if your child is having a hard time because you said 'no' to buying a new toy, you can say something like, "I would really like to buy a new TV for the living room, but we can't spend all that money right now. I'll have to start saving some money little by little so maybe we can buy a new TV in a few months."

Use "I Know" Statements - The word 'no' can sound harsh to parents, especially if they're not used to using it. But there are many ways to say 'no' with empathy, care, and understanding. Try using "I Know" statements to help your child understand that you're there to help them through their difficult emotions like, "I know you're wanting to go outside and that you're upset, but you must pick up these blocks first," or "I know that you don't want to eat, but my job is to make sure you stay healthy, so let's eat our dinner together." Remember, saying 'no' doesn't mean you're uncaring. On the contrary, it means that you love your child enough to teach them important lessons about respect, selflessness, and responsibility.

Teach Gratitude - When you help your child focus on all the wonderful people, things, and experiences that are already in his or her life, you'll create an environment where they are thankful for what they already have. The simple question of, "What are you thankful for today?" can become a beautiful ritual before bed or around the dinner table. It also allows children to focus on all the wonderful things they have in their lives and the people that go out of their way to do so much for them.

***

"Saying yes to everything your child asks for is often easier than saying no. But no, while more exhausting, will eventually teach your child important life lessons. You and your child will reap the benefits later on."
- Lyn, Teacher

"I think parents have to remember they are the adult and have to set guidelines. It's ok to say no."
- Alice, Retired Early Childhood Teacher

TOYS

Why the best toys for children today
have actually been around for decades

> *"I once bought my kids a set of batteries for Christmas with a note on it saying, 'Toys Not Included.'"* - Bernard Manning

It's easy for parents to feel overwhelmed when it comes to choosing toys for their children. There are so many options, many with bright lights, music, technology-enabled features, and extensive instructions. Ads for these toys are everywhere, with many boasting impressive educational benefits. This isn't surprising considering the toy industry has now reached one billion dollars worldwide. [lxxix] Parents are inundated with messages about new toys that will give their child a leg up, but often these toys overpromise and under deliver...and eventually end up collecting dust on a shelf.

So are there actually toys that will help children learn and be fun for them to play with at the same time? Jeffrey Trawick-Smith, Professor of Early Childhood Education at Eastern Connecticut State University, studies toys and their role in a child's development. He believes that there are educationally and developmentally engaging toys...but they don't require batteries or syncing anything to a Bluetooth enabled device. He discovered that simple, open-ended toys like wooden blocks, toy vehicles, and building sets seem to offer the most opportunities for learning. Open-ended toys are ones that spark a child's play using imagination and creativity. He states, "These toys are relatively open-ended, so children can use them in multiple ways. Also, they have all been around for a long time. There may be a reason these toys have been enjoyed by children over the generations!"[lxxx]

In the years I've spent in preschool classrooms, I've identified several types of toys that keep children engaged, develop creativity, and stimulate the senses. Many are quite inexpensive or cost nothing at all! Most are not new, but have stood the test of time by pleasing children for many years. So if you're feeling stumped about what toys will be best for your child, consider items in these categories to promote learning and discovery:

***

YOU'VE GOT THIS!

Blocks of All Kinds - For very young children, try foam blocks, which are larger and softer. As children grow, try hardwood, hollow, and inch wooden blocks to promote open-ended design and also improve dexterity and fine motor control. Basic DUPLO and LEGO blocks that allow children to free-build and experiment are also great options.

Sensory Exploration Materials - Materials that children can touch, squeeze, pour, and pinch are wonderful for allowing them to explore with their senses. Play-dough is one of the best options, and I particularly love the homemade kind using cream of tartar. There are many recipes available online and you can involve your child in making it with you in the kitchen. Sand, kinetic sand, water, or water beads in a sensory bin are also wonderful options that promote open-ended learning experiences and sensory development.

Dramatic Play Items - Children love to reenact situations that they see in their lives by acting out roles or pretending to be someone else. Items that can assist in fun dramatic play experiences include dress-up clothes, wooden toy kitchen items and play food, and toy tools. You can even find some dramatic play items right outside your door: Children love using sticks for pasta and rocks for meatballs!

Simple Structures - Wooden barns and dollhouses are great for letting children design special spaces for small figures.

Construction Sets - Toy construction sets are particularly fun. Children love to build railroads, streets, and buildings.

Magna-Tiles are especially popular and my grandson loves using these to build garages for his toy cars or skyscrapers for his super hero figures.

Art Materials - Don't overlook the benefits of a simple sheet of paper and some crayons or markers. There are millions of ways children can turn these simple materials into new creations...then want to do it over and over again.

Board Games - Even though board games are not open-ended, they are extremely beneficial in helping children develop social-emotional skills and awareness. Games like *Candy Land* and *Chutes and Ladders* are wonderful because they teach children about taking turns, playing with others, and being a good winner or loser.

Toys That Cost Nothing at All - Don't forget: There are many open-ended play experiences for children that don't require you to purchase anything at all! A sheet over a table can become a fun fort! A large box can become a playhouse! Two wooden spoons and an upside down pot can become a drum set! Get creative with the items you already have around your house. Many times those become more popular than the expensive toys from the store!

THE UPSIDE OF
DIGITAL DEVICES

How family screen time can make your child
more screen smart, literate, and empathetic

> *"We need to break the old mold of 'media policing' and create new ways of interacting with our children around screens that will support rather than erode family dynamics."* - Nicole Dreiske

For decades parents have been warned and have worried about the impact of technology on their children, especially in early childhood. Today, tech insiders are saying that software developers make their products purposely addictive and the World Health Organization just classified "addiction to gaming" as an actual disease. What's the solution? We all know the regular drill: limit screen time and monitor what our kids watch and play. But are those really our best and only tools?

Nicole Dreiske's *Screen Smart™* approach builds on strengths parents already have to help children develop healthy screen habits. To start that process, she asked hundreds of parents and teachers how they want their children to interact with screens. "What does a great relationship with screens look like in early childhood? How can screen time support our children educationally and developmentally?"

Parents told her that they wanted their children to come to them when they're upset or have questions about things they see on screens. They wanted children to know when "enough is enough" and screens should be turned off. Teachers longed for children to notice "the story in a movie" and use "story vocabulary" when watching screens.

Taking that feedback, Dreiske created the *Screen Smart*™ method to fulfill those "wish lists" and field-tested the techniques with thousands of kids, teachers and parents. Here are her tips for developing *Screen Smart*™ skills and transforming screen time. The key is to connect the stories we read in books, to the stories children see on screens.

***

YOU'VE GOT THIS!

Before viewing, "prime" the child for this fun, new way of using screens. Try saying, "Today we're going to do something special and watch/play together! We're going to look for what we like, what we don't like, and why." Or you can say, "We're going to notice what we're feeling and thinking while we're watching."

Use your "storybook voice" to interact with your child during or after screen time once or twice a week. When using digital devices together, you can encourage, coax, and tease out answers the way you do when reading books aloud. While you're watching or holding the screen, take time to enjoy the shared space and the cuddling, using a playful and caring tone. Using "storybook skills" when watching screens with your little ones is comforting for children and strengthens family bonds.

Point out details, share ideas, and ask questions. While you're reading a storybook, a child may ask a question, or point out a color, or an object, or a character they enjoy. You contribute whimsical comments and queries, perhaps tying real life experiences to the book. If a child points to the picture of a dog and says, "Puppy!" you might say, "Yes, we saw a dog at the park today! What color was the dog we saw? What color is this dog?" That same kind of interaction can easily take place during shared viewing. Every word counts in early childhood and the more words shared with parents, the better!

Continue the dialogue! After screen time, talk with your children, asking what part of the movie or game they liked and why. If a child asks you what happened, try turning the question back – "What do you think happened here?" The trick is to avoid passive viewing. Talking together about movies, TV, Internet and electronic games is a natural extension of positive family communications. Plus it helps your children develop the skills they need for success in the 21st century.

-Content in this section provided by Nicole Dreiske. She is an educational innovator, children's media expert, and the author of *THE UPSIDE OF DIGITAL DEVICES: How to Make Your Child More Screen Smart,™ Literate and Emotionally Intelligent.*

WHINING

How to teach your child to thoughtfully
and calmly express themselves

> *"When it comes to torture, we could all learn a thing or two from kids. Who knows better than they how to extract most anything they want within minutes of applying the technique? I'm talking about whining, of course -- that grating mewling that causes us to do anything (anything!) just to make it go away."*- Julie Tilsner

Whining can start as soon as children have the language to express their disdain for not getting their way. Whining can stem from a child not wanting to clean up toys, having to go to bed, or from something as seemingly benign as being given the wrong color of socks to put on. Even though whining can be especially exhausting for parents, it's actually incredibly important that they show their children that life won't always hand them everything they want as soon as they want it...and that whining won't change that. As one mother recently told me, "As my children grow my biggest concern for them is helping them know that everything in life does not always go as you may plan it to be and that's ok. I want to give them the tools to manage their expectations."

In order to help young children begin to learn these tools, it's first important to consider why the whining is occurring in the first place. Dr. Jessica Michaelson states that many children may whine because they legitimately need help or resources from a parent. She suggests whining often lets children communicate that they're not feeling well, are overwhelmed, or simply "can't act big anymore." [lxxxi] But developmental psychologist Becky Bailey notes that whining can also be a child's cry for more connection with a parent: "Ask yourself, 'Have I been busier than usual? Has my child's routine changed? Has a sibling required more attention for some reason?' Often, whining is a signal it's time to reconnect with your child."[lxxxii]

Regardless of the cause of your child's whining, it's important that parents handle it in a calm manner. If you raise your voice or let your temper get the best of you, the whining will only intensify. Instead, model a calm voice and engage in conversation to show your child that words can express feelings better than whining.

Remember to look for the root of the whining and try these tips to minimize it in the future:

***

YOU'VE GOT THIS!

Teach your child that you will listen when he or she uses a regular voice. The Center for Parenting Education states, "When your child first starts to whine, you can say, 'I cannot hear you when you whine. You need to use a regular voice to tell me what you want.'"[lxxxiii] Repeat this statement if the whining continues and even demonstrate what a "regular voice" sounds like. Let your child know that you can't understand what he or she wants if they aren't able to speak as usual, which encourages him or her to stop and regain calm before trying again.

Recognize your child's progress when he or she shows restraint and uses regular speech. Use statements like, "I was able to hear you when you used your normal, pleasant voice," or "My ears are very happy to hear that tone of voice." This will let your child know that you acknowledge his or her efforts to make progress, which can also dramatically decrease occurrences of future whining.

Teach delayed gratification and show empathy to nip whining in the bud. For example, if your child wants to get a big box of cookies at the grocery store, and you see a struggle on the horizon, first show empathy by saying something like, "Those do look good, don't they?" But then follow up by proposing a situation that shows the child that he or she can have patience and doesn't need the desired item instantly: "We're in charge of bringing snacks to your art class next week. Would you like to get some cookies then to share with your friends?" This can then lead your child to brainstorm other snacks. The same can happen with a toy: Ask your child, "Would you like to add this to your birthday wish list or earn money to buy it yourself?" These situations don't just delay gratification and help stop impending whining, but they also encourage children to make thoughtful decisions.

IN CONCLUSION

"In today's age the goal of a parent is to make sure their child faces no obstacle, challenge, or heartache. They think when their child faces disappointment, anger, or pain (both emotional and physical) it is because they made a mistake as a parent. What should be expressed and taught is that things happen in life. These things that happen are neither good nor bad; it's just life. Your child is not immune to them, everyone faces them, and the only thing that matters is how you respond to them. Most of the time the parent or child can't control the situation, but they can control their attitude, how to look at the situation, and their ability to show resolve and fight for better days. The only thing a parent should promise the child is that when 'life happens' they won't be alone. They are cared for and loved and are prepared for these situations through faith, family, and friends. There will always be someone to look after them and one day when they get older, wiser, and stronger, they will be the ones looking after others."

- Jamie, Director of Business Development, Nutrition Wellness Center

ABOUT THE AUTHOR

Christine Kyriakakos Martin has extensive experience and expertise in the fields of child development and early childhood education. She received her B.A. in Child Study from St. Joseph's College in Hartford, CT, and a Master of Science degree in Early Childhood Education from Wheelock College in Boston, MA.

Christine is passionate about children's positive growth and development; days spent with children are her happiest ones. Learning about them, how they learn, how they think, what is most fun for them, and exploring the world through their eyes has brought her years of joy. The most rewarding part of her professional career has been teaching children and adults.

Christine is the founder and owner of Sunshine Preschool in Hopkinton, MA, a NAEYC nationally accredited program, which has been in operation for over 40 years. She is also the co-founder of the St. Spyridon's Nursery school in Worcester, MA. She acted as a reviewer for the State of Massachusetts to approve continuing education courses for teaching professionals and served as a trainer for both the Massachusetts Department of Education for Early Childhood Programs and Standards and the Systematic Training for Effective Parenting (STEP) program. Christine has also been a featured speaker on child development issues and early childhood topics at colleges and at NAEYC national conventions across the country.

Christine is currently an educational consultant and serves on the Board of Directors of the International Children's Media Center, an organization dedicated to changing the way children view, use, and engage with media.

She has 3 children: Nick, Jamie, and Ashley and one grandchild, Austin. She currently resides in Florida with her husband, Jim.

ACKNOWLEDGEMENTS

Thank you to the following contributors that offered their time, shared their memories, and provided words of wisdom and encouragement throughout this book: Renee Angelosante, Alice Bartlett, Lyn Calkins, Janica Caster, Darrin Caster, Liz Dacey, Heidi Davis, Bill DiBenedetto, Molly Di Benedetto, Yvonne DiBenedetto, Nicole Dreiske, Gabriela Dunn, Kevin Dunn, Maryellen Faroni, Russell Faroni, Jackie Finn, Tom Fitzpatrick, Athena Fitzpatrick, Matthew Fitzpatrick, Justin Hawkins, Doug Horton, Ashley Horton, Missy Jenkins, Jamie Kyriakakos, Nick Kyriakakos, Nicole Matty, Ginnie Pace, Carol Quinlan, Sharon Richardson, Katie Rizi, Linda Rosen, Lauren Schuth, Lisa Summers, Irene Tsoules, Evans Tsoules, Robin White, Pat White, and Heather York.

ENDNOTE REFERENCES AND LINKS

[i] Riley, Dave, et al. (2008). *Social & Emotional Development*. St. Paul: Redleaf.

[ii] Riley, P. 13

[iii] Riley, P.15

[iv] https://centerforparentingeducation.org/library-of-articles/nutrition-and-healthy-lifestyle/sleep-kids-adults-we-are-all-grouchy-without-enough/

[v] http://www.easternflorida.edu/community-resources/child-development-centers/parent-resource-library/documents/beat-bedtime-blues.pdf

[vi] http://nieer.org/wp-content/uploads/2016/08/16.pdf

[vii] http://nieer.org/wp-content/uploads/2016/08/16.pdf

[viii] http://raisingchildren.net.au/articles/consequences.html#natural

[ix] http://raisingchildren.net.au/articles/consequences.html#natural

[x] https://www.huffingtonpost.com/2013/08/02/disability-awareness-parents-teach-kids_n_3696279.html

[xi] http://www.pbs.org/parents/experts/archive/2009/02/teaching-children-about-divers.html#

[xii] https://www.huffingtonpost.ca/craig-and-marc-kielburger/diverse-toys-children_b_14283280.html

[xiii] https://www.independent.co.uk/life-style/health-and-families/children-picky-eaters-genetics-parents-fussy-study-food-university-illinois-usa-a8112131.html

[xiv] https://www.parenting.com/article/picky-eater-kids

[xv] https://www.independent.co.uk/life-style/health-and-families/children-picky-eaters-genetics-parents-fussy-study-food-university-illinois-usa-a8112131.html

[xvi] https://www.parenting.com/article/picky-eater-kids

[xvii] http://msue.anr.msu.edu/news/praise_vs_encouragement

[xviii] https://www.nytimes.com/2011/08/13/your-money/childrens-activities-no-guarantee-of-later-success.html

[xix] https://www.nytimes.com/2011/08/13/your-money/childrens-activities-no-guarantee-of-later-success.html

[xx] http://living.thebump.com/family-impact-early-childhood-development-10352.html

xxi http://living.thebump.com/family-impact-early-childhood-development-10352.html

xxii https://www.merriam-webster.com/dictionary/quality%20time?src=search-dict-box

xxiii https://www.parents.com/parenting/better-parenting/positive/quality-time/

xxiv https://www.brightfutures.org/mentalhealth/pdf/families/ec/fears.pdf

xxv https://www.babycenter.com/0_preschool-fears-why-they-happen-and-what-to-do_64094.bc?page=2&articleId=64094

xxvi http://kidshealth.org/en/parents/anxiety.html?WT.ac=ctg#catfeelings

xxvii https://www.psychologytoday.com/us/blog/psyched/201402/fine-motor-skills-and-academic-achievement

xxviii https://www.washingtonpost.com/news/parenting/wp/2016/07/25/the-importance-of-childhood-friendships-and-how-to-nurture-them/?noredirect=on&utm_term=.6a246533499b

xxix http://www.scholastic.com/browse/article.jsp?id=3747174

xxx https://childdevelopment.com.au/areas-of-concern/gross-motor-skills/gross-motor-skills/

xxxi http://www.peacefulplaygrounds.com/download/pdf/Physical%20Fitness%20and%20Academic%20Achievement%20in%20Third%20and%20Fifth%20Grade%20Students.pdf

xxxii http://csefel.vanderbilt.edu/kits/wwbtk3.pdf

xxxiii http://www.hanen.org/Helpful-Info/Articles/Power-of-Using-Everyday-Routines.aspx

xxxiv http://nocrysolution.com/books/the-no-cry-discipline-solution-2/interrupting/

xxxv http://www.pbs.org/parents/experts/archive/2011/08/helping-children-prepare-for-k.html

xxxvi http://www.readingrockets.org/webcasts/1002

xxxvii https://www.scholastic.com/parents/books-and-reading/language-and-speech/meaning-preliteracy.html

xxxviii http://www.readingrockets.org/webcasts/1002

xxxix https://www.theguardian.com/commentisfree/2014/dec/15/children-lie-age-two-tell-truth

xl https://www.theguardian.com/commentisfree/2014/dec/15/children-lie-age-two-tell-truth

xli https://www.parenting.com/article/why-kids-lie-age-by-age

xlii https://www.parenting.com/article/why-kids-lie-age-by-age

xliii https://www.bostonglobe.com/magazine/2004/11/07/all-talked-out/02noDArKRdmquSEctwov5N/story.html xliv https://www.bostonglobe.com/magazine/2004/11/07/all-talked-out/02noDArKRdmquSEctwov5N/story.html

xlv http://www.chicagotribune.com/lifestyles/parenting/sc-fam-quality-time-kids-parenting-1219-story.html

xlvi https://www.parentingforbrain.com/4-baumrind-parenting-styles/

xlvii https://www.parentingforbrain.com/4-baumrind-parenting-styles/

xlviii https://www.naeyc.org/resources/pubs/yc/may2017/case-brain-science-guided-play

xlix https://www.naeyc.org/resources/pubs/yc/may2017/case-brain-science-guided-play

l http://www.essentialkids.com.au/development-advice/development/encouraging-children-to-ask-questions-20140112-30pfa

li http://www.trelease-on-reading.com/read-aloud-brochure.pdf

lii http://www.reachoutandread.org/FileRepository/ReadingAloudtoChildren_ADC_July2008.pdf

liii https://www.thenational.ae/arts-culture/why-the-first-five-years-of-a-child-s-development-are-the-most-important-1.127401

liv https://medium.com/thrive-global/will-technology-ruin-your-childrens-development-663351c76974

lv http://healthland.time.com/2012/07/20/pediatricians-call-on-the-fcc-to-reconsider-cell-phone-radiation-standards/

lvi https://www.thenational.ae/arts-culture/why-the-first-five-years-of-a-child-s-development-are-the-most-important-1.127401

lvii https://www.thenational.ae/arts-culture/why-the-first-five-years-of-a-child-s-development-are-the-most-important-1.127401

lviii Dreiske, Nicole, *The Upside of Digital Devices: How to Make Your Child More Screen Smart, Literate, and Emotionally Intelligent.* Deerfield Beach, FL: HCI Books, 2018.

lix https://my.vanderbilt.edu/developmentalpsychologyblog/2013/12/instilling-self-esteem-in-children/

lx https://my.vanderbilt.edu/developmentalpsychologyblog/2013/12/instilling-self-esteem-in-children/

lxi https://my.vanderbilt.edu/developmentalpsychologyblog/2013/12/instilling-self-esteem-in-children/

lxii http://kidshealth.org/en/parents/sep-anxiety.html?ref=search&WT.ac=msh-p-dtop-en-search-clk#catfeelings

lxiii http://www.ahaparenting.com/parenting-tools/siblings/Teach-Share-Sharing

lxiv http://www.ahaparenting.com/parenting-tools/siblings/Teach-Share-Sharing

[lxv] Eisenberg, Nancy. "Eight Tips to Developing Caring Kids" in David Streight (Ed). (2009). Good Things To Do: Expert Suggestions for Fostering Goodness in Kids Portland: The Center for Spiritual and Ethical Education

[lxvi] https://www.parents.com/toddlers-preschoolers/development/social/how-to-help-your-shy-child/

[lxvii] https://www.kidsinthehouse.com/elementary/social-life/friends/helping-shy-or-introverted-child?qt-more_videos=1#qt-more_videos

[lxviii] https://www.kidsinthehouse.com/elementary/social-life/how-help-your-shy-child-make-friends?qt-more_videos=1#qt-more_videos

[lxix] http://www.ahaparenting.com/parenting-tools/siblings/great-sibling-relationship-from-the-start

[lxx] https://www.nytimes.com/2018/05/08/smarter-living/how-to-maintain-sibling-relationships.html

[lxxi] https://www.focusonthefamily.com/parenting/building-relationships/sibling-rivalry/sibling-rivalry-teaching-kids-to-be-kind

[lxxii] Epstein, Anne S., *Me, You, Us: Social-Emotional Learning in Preschool.* Ypsilanti, MI: Highscope, 2000.

[lxxiii] http://pediatrics.aappublications.org/content/119/1/182

[lxxiv] http://pediatrics.aappublications.org/content/119/1/182

[lxxv] https://www.fatherly.com/health-science/the-science-behind-superhero-play-and-childhood-development/

[lxxvi] http://www.easternflorida.edu/community-resources/child-development-centers/parent-resource-library/documents/parenting-the-difficult-temperament.pdf

[lxxvii] http://www.pa-pat.org/wp-content/uploads/sites/9/2016/06/HANDOUT-Nine-Temperament-Traits-Three-Temperament-Types.pdf

[lxxviii] https://www.scholastic.com/parents/family-life/parent-child/its-okay-to-say-no.html

[lxxix] https://www.statista.com/topics/1108/toy-industry/

[lxxx] https://www.naeyc.org/resources/topics/play/specific-toys-play

[lxxxi] https://www.mother.ly/child/the-science-behind-why-kids-whine

[lxxxii] https://www.webmd.com/parenting/features/why-kids-whine-and-how-to-stop-them

[lxxxiii] https://centerforparentingeducation.org/parentscorner/ry